THE CHURCH IN PERSPECTIVE

Standard Lay Reader's Training Course

by
Edmund B. Partridge

Morehouse-Barlow Co.
Wilton, Connecticut 06897

Third Printing 1982
© 1969 by Morehouse-Barlow Co.
Revised and updated 1976
Library of Congress Catalog Card No. 68—56918
ISBN - 0-8192-1210-5

Printed in the United States of America

To Harold Raymond Partridge

Contents

Introduction 1

I. Church History 3

II. The Development of Christian Theology 41

III. Liturgical Worship 63

IV. The Ecumenical Situation 85

V. The Role of the Lay Reader 95

INTRODUCTION

One of the oldest offices in the Church is the office of lay reader. Its roots lie in the synagogue worship of the Old Testament along with much else now a part of the Christian heritage. The New Testament record makes clear that St. Paul regularly preached in the synagogues even before his apostolate was officially sanctioned by the young church, and St. Luke tells us that Jesus "taught in their synagogues..." "and he stood up to read..." (St. Luke 4:15, 16). As Bishop Stephen Bayne pointed out in *The Guide for Lay Readers*, our Lord himself can be understood, in part, in terms of the typical role of laymen in Old Testament Jewry, which gave us the model for the role of lay reader.

The Christian faith is often described in the imagery of warfare. Indeed, in baptism we are pledged to serve as Christ's faithful soldiers. In similar terms, it is not an overstatement to characterize lay readers as the church's reserve officers; they can and do provide the faithful with corporate public worship.

Because the office of lay reader is an ancient one, it has undergone some changes. Today that office, like all the orders

2 INTRODUCTION

of ministry, is going through a period of further development. Indeed, it continues to change in the Episcopal Church, for at the General Convention in Seattle, Washington, in September 1967, the Canon on Lay Readers (Canon 49) was amended to permit certain authorized lay readers to administer the chalice at Holy Communion. That amendment brings American practice into alignment with the more ancient role of lay readers in the Church of England. There is every reason to look for other developments; the Knowledge Revolution has given this age an unparalleled degree of sophistication. In a tradition committed to the principle of an educated ministry rather than a ministry qualified by divine inspiration alone, lay readers have been among the last to benefit from the capability the Church is able to bestow upon them. In the face of the greater demands made upon the lay reader's individual ability, however, this situation is rapidly changing. Recognizing that no amount of piety can make up for a dearth of knowledge, some lay readers have become lay theologians of repute, and all recognize that to do their work adequately a wide range of special knowledge and ability is required. Thus, the lay reader is joining the clergy in the ranks of the Church's educated leaders.

This work is offered in the hope that it will meet the educational needs of lay readers and other church members desiring a brief survey of the church's history, theology, and liturgics.

The explicit purpose of the Standard Lay Readers' Training Course is to give an overview of all the academic material required by Canon 49, "Of Lay Readers." This text will provide content for individual or group use adequate for qualification as an Episcopal lay reader. The arrangement of the subject matter is such that the book can be used readily for reference and review.

E.B.P.
New York, N.Y.
1976

I. CHURCH HISTORY

Early History of Israel

Had Christ come into human history before "the fulness of time," his coming would *not* have been misconstrued by many and rejected by most, but would have gone unnoticed. Briefly stated, the history of Israel before the birth of Christ was God's preparation of the world for his supreme self-revelation in the person of Christ.

Probably, most people believe that the monotheism of Israel started with a "burning bush." Actually, the progress from polytheism, or the worship of many gods, to monotheism, or the belief in one universal god, went through a stage highly relevant to our own day, a stage of belief called *monolatry*. There is a charming little story told in II Kings 5, which illustrates monolatry.

Naaman, the Syrian army commander, had contracted leprosy, which was no less feared in that century than cancer is today. Told by one of his slaves of the ability of the prophet Elisha to heal diseases, Naaman went to the prophet in Israel and was so impressed with the healing miracle performed upon him by Elisha, "the man of God," that he decided henceforth to worship only the God by whose power Elisha had accomplished the cure. So the Syrian army commander went to Elisha and said, "Behold, I know there is no God in all the earth, but in Israel...let there be given to your servant two mules' burden of (Israel's) earth; for henceforth your servant will not offer burnt offering or sacrifice to any god but the Lord" (II Kings 5:15, 17).

Monolatry is the worship of one god. It does not require disbelief in other gods but carries with it the notion that every god is *geographically* limited in the same way that a king, governor, or bishop is. Thus, the Jews could put their own faith in Yahweh and still believe that other gods existed, since these other gods each had a territory or sphere of influence.

Monolatry is still with us today. It is implicit in questions like the astral discovery question: If intelligent beings were discovered on some other planet, would Christ be their Lord? Obviously, if Christ is the self-expressive aspect of the Creator-God, and that is what we mean by our credal assertions that through Christ "all things were made," then wherever the Creator's works are to be found, there, too, is the Lordship of Christ.

Although monotheism came somewhat later in the history of Israel than monolatry, this was *not* a natural progression; it does not follow that polytheism leads through monolatry to monotheism. Monotheism was not developed out of polytheism but in opposition to it.

The significant lessons the Jews had to learn in preparation for Christ's coming were (1) that there is one Lord who rules over all creation and (2) that faith in the God of the universe must be highly ethical. These two lessons were learned only gradually, over the course of many centuries. Isaiah gave to Israel (see story of Uzziah, Isaiah 6) the concept that holiness, always thought of as physical, must be ethical as well. In like manner, the universal rule of God, which we think of today as essential to a monotheistic outlook, came sometime before the fifth century B.C. We cannot date precisely the first real acceptance of God's universal rule. All we can say with absolute certainty is that monotheism appeared sometime between Moses and II Isaiah (see section on Holy Scriptures). By the time of II Isaiah, about 540 B.C., monotheism was the orthodox, conventional, established faith of Israel.

The history of Israel is the preparation of a certain people by God for his ultimate self-revelation. Monotheism existed elsewhere, in Egypt and Mesopotamia, and the more significant fact about the Hebrews was that they were, as we say, "the Chosen People." Why did God choose the Jews? Perhaps the best answer is that they alone chose him. Their religious vocation was a two-way affair. They "married" God, so to speak. Over and over again they liken their relationship with God to marriage (see the book of Hosea, which is entirely constructed around such an analogy). Much as the church is the bride of Christ, the Chosen People of Israel were united with God.

It seems in the light of our best evidence that Israel worshiped one god as early as the Patriarchal Period (2000 to 1500 B.C.). In the book of Genesis, we read that he had many names, for example: El Shadden (Exodus 6:3; Genesis 17:1), El Elyan (Genesis 14:18), El Olam (Genesis 21:23), and so on. This patriarchal religion was the milieu in which Yahwism developed, but it was not the same as later monotheism. First, it was a territorial religion—a monolatry. Moreover, it was not ethical in any way that approaches the present use of the word. Yahwism, or later Hebrew monotheism, developed under Moses after the Jews fled Egypt. Although the Exodus cannot be dated, reliable biblical scholars place it in the thirteenth century B.C. It may well be that Moses' own belief in one god was largely Egyptian inspired, for a monotheism flourished there under Pharaoh Amenhotep IV Iknahton, in the fifteenth century B.C. In preaching Yahwism, Moses was behaving just as patriarchs have always done: each patriarch before Moses had had a "patron god" and all his people were loyal to that god, whom they referred to as "the god of their father," because the patriarch was the father of the clan. At Sinai, Moses was acting as the patriarch of *all* the Hebrews, not just one family or clan.

We must not pass over his accomplishment too lightly. Moses molded his people into a single unit—a nation—which could then be loyal to one god. Without this "national unification," the Jews would probably never have gone beyond a highly refined monolatry to the ethical monotheism that we associate with them. When Moses established the worship of Yahweh among the Jews, these people looked for historic justification of their faith. Finding that all the former patriarchs had worshiped a patron god, they simply identified all those patron gods as Yahweh called by other names. Thus, to the Hebrew after the Exodus, Yahweh was "the God of Abraham, the God of Isaac, and the God of Jacob" (Exodus 3:6).

From the time of the Exodus to the time of the united Kingdom of Israel, or roughly from 1280 to 970 B.C., the nation was a confederation of tribes united by their covenant (or contracted relationship) with Yahweh. This stage of Israel's history is like the manner in which the Anglican Communion today is united—a confederation of autonomous churches (like tribes) in communion with (covenanted to) the See of Canterbury. The religious center of the tribal confederacy was the shrine and the Ark of the Covenant. This period of Hebrew history is described in the Book of Judges. There was no central government overall, only local judges. Invariably, when outside enemies threatened, there arose a judge of sufficient stature to unite and lead the nation. This kind of leadership had neither traditional responsibilities nor any real power or succession. All the leader or judge had was a following held by the attractive force of his personality. The people regarded God as their king, and they understood themselves to be a theocratic nation, a nation ruled by God. Although the shrine that housed the Ark of the Covenant was central in this religious scheme, its location was not permanent or fixed. There were, in fact, several famous religious centers in ancient Israel, frequently named in the Bible. Among them are Bethel, Shechem, Gilgal, and Shiloh. Each was the center of the area's cultic (that is religio-social) life.

Israel Under the Judges

It is almost impossible to exaggerate the significance of Moses' accomplishment in molding the twelve tribes of Israel into one nation. Moses was not a dictator in the modern sense of the word, but he was able to bring about, by the means dictators have always used, a totalitarian state whose diverse elements were cemented together by a loyalty to God not unlike nationalism or patriotism in its effectiveness. Moses created a god-centered people (not a place-centered or race-centered one as in the case of nationalism). They were a theocracy, a kingdom whose ruler was God. In the beginning, theocracy was essentially *monolatry*, not monotheism. The religious expression the people gave to God's rule was a fanatic dependence, which carried with it a crude sense of divine meddling, as it were. God was thought to be the cause of everything that happened. He not only blessed, he cursed. And he was absolutely dependable in doing so. Having given Israel its law, the Commandments, he promised its people bane or blessing, pain or sorrow, according to their just desserts.

There is a valid principle here—God does provide for his people and is responsive to the conscientious efforts of people who are trying to be good by providing for their deepest needs. Therefore, the moral principle that human behavior has meaning—and consequences as well—has a religious basis.

The Israelites of Old Testament times, however, missed this deeper significance of the Law and, in missing it, their concept of God became distorted. They reasoned that since God alone can bless or curse, any who suffer must deserve suffering and any who have good luck must be righteous. The self-righteous Pharisees in Christ's Parable of the Pharisee and the Publican (see St. Luke 18) illustrate the attitude characteristic of all but the latter days of the Old Testament age about rewards and punishments in this life. Quite possibly—and very reasonably, in view of the Old Testament faith about these things—the Pharisee came into the Temple deeply moved by gratitude for some benefit a kindly Providence has bestowed. Seeing in the Temple a man whose very profession was hateful to the Jews, and perhaps noticing some obvious affliction in that man, the Pharisee would naturally compare himself, as righteous and therefore blessed, to the obviously unrighteous and therefore not so blessed man beside him. The Pharisee's spiritual blindness was more the fault of others, or the system in which he was brought up, than his own, for this is what the Israelites were taught to believe about God.

Moses had brought all of Israel to God, and such a capable leader is not easily replaced. For centuries after his death, there was no one of comparable stature and ability to succeed him. Although Joshua, who succeeded Moses as the leader of Israel and defeated the people of Canaan, was an uncommonly good general, Moses left a nation of united, highly confident, dedicated people, whereas Joshua had the misfortune to preside over a shocking religious decline. This decline is well illustrated by the famous and fabled battle of Jericho (Joshua 5:13 ff). God is given credit for the victory, but to "honor" him, the victorious Israelites committed the atrocity of slaughtering all the captives! This is crude religion, but from a strictly pragmatic point of view, it was a useful means of conquest. The "Promised Land" upon which Joshua entered was not a unified nation but a varied group of racially related people, grouped loosely around central cities like Jericho. The inhabitants of the land (then called the Land of Canaan, later Palestine, and now divided between the states of Israel and Jordan) were no more than a loose confederation of city-states. Probably, a more unified country would have resisted the invading Israelites successfully.

The conquest of Canaan under Joshua and his successors was a gradual process, which inevitably involved the assimilation of the conquered inhabitants. This took place as the natural result of living together and intermarrying, but it produced a serious dilution and corruption of the Mosaic faith by the assimilation of certain pagan cultic practices (human sacrifice, for example). Chapter 24 of the Book of Joshua serves as a good example of this transitional period of the conquest. It relates Joshua's calling together "all the tribes of Israel" at Shechem and confronting them with three religious realities: (1) God had formed the Chosen People, had delivered them from Egyptian bondage, and had brought them to the Promised Land, (2) this God that delivered them deserved their love and their gratitude, and (3) Joshua would serve that God and worship him: his service and worship would be the living testimony of his love and loyalty.

Joshua then renewed the Covenant with God at Shechem (one of the cultic centers of religious worship before the days of King David, under whom worship became centralized in Jerusalem), and that renewal took the form of an elaborate religious ceremony (described in Joshua 24).

The god pictured in the book of Joshua appears at the most cursory glance to be a god whose ways are war and violence, yet this understanding is shaped by events, as most theology is. The religious faith of the people may often say more about them than about the God who is the object of their faith. To the Israelites, involved in conquest, only a "war god" made sense. Their war-god faith met the demands of their religious need and in turn made sense out of their worldly experience. The element that changes in the unfolding revelation of the Scriptures is not God, but man's perception of him.

☦ ☦ ☦ ☦ ☦

We have now seen how Moses united the people of Israel into a God-centered nation and how, as a result of mixing with the peoples they conquered, their religion took on foreign, pagan elements. There did remain, however, the Mosaic Law and the nation, which, though it often fell into sin, never openly repudiated the Law. After the conquest of Canaan, the next stage in the pre-Christian history of our heritage comes with the period of the Judges, of whom Joshua was the first.

The best available date for the beginning of the period of the Judges is the middle of the twelfth century B.C., or roughly a century after Moses. As the invading Israelites settled down to the life of farming that they found already developed by the conquered people of Canaan—a big adjustment for the formerly nomadic, wandering Israelite—their attention centered more and more on their local concerns and less on outside threats. Occasionally, those whom they had conquered attempted rebellion, and we read repeatedly of wars with Canaanites, Perisites, Hittites, and other neighbors. The story of Deborah (Judges 4 and 5) and Jael and Sisera tells of one such Canaanite uprising.

The period of the Judges is critical in the history of the Israelites because during it they accomplished the tasks by which their national identity was preserved. The period of the Judges is relatively short (about 1150-1050 B.C.), but in that space of time the nation conquered the Promised Land and its people put down their roots. They also assimilated the conquered Canaanite peoples, taking into their own culture many religious practices of the Canaanites. We have already seen that the Judges ruled by the force of their personalities and generally only long enough to deal with an emergency, such as an attack from a local neighboring tribe. Finally, however, an enemy loomed on their coast far more terrible than any they had faced. This was the Philistines, a seafaring people unusually sophisticated at warfare. Settling on the Mediterranean Coast between Gaza and Mt. Carmel, they came in contact with the new inhabitants of Palestine and had frequent skirmishes with them. Clearly, what was needed was stronger central government and, in the world of that day, monarchy was the typical form of centralized rule. Although there are gaps in our knowledge of the religious life of the nation at this time, it is certain that the worship of Yahweh was a vital force in the nation's life.

The Monarchy

The history of the Monarchy is the story of three kings, Saul, David, and Solomon. The best of them was David, while perhaps the most pathetic was Saul, the first of the three to occupy the throne. Saul was anointed king by Samuel at a difficult time. Not only was the Philistine threat imminent but also the times were transitional: the nation was only beginning to assume organization. The date is hard to set with precision, but 1050 B.C. is close. Saul appears to have been going insane even at the outset of his reign. During his fits of depression, the young shepherd musician David would soothe him with music and song (I Samuel 16:14ff). David's popularity was enormously sudden, especially after he slew the Philistine giant, Goliath (I Samuel 17), and, thereafter, Saul despised David and jealously sought to kill him. The prophet Samuel anointed David king to rule in Saul's place.

Undoubtedly, David was a great king. More difficult to assess than his secular greatness is his religious significance. Perhaps even more than any other man, Moses included, he made the Chosen People function as a nation. They had found at Moses' hands a common faith in Yahweh and a common concern for their corporate destiny, but no one before David made them conscious of a national life bound up with land, government, tradition, heritage—and pride! David made Israel nationally self-conscious, and one means by which he did so was to establish a central religious sanctuary at Jerusalem.

Before King David's victory, Jerusalem (undoubtedly the "Salem" mentioned in Genesis 14) was a pagan stronghold, which resisted capture during the conquest that Joshua led. Joshua 15:63 relates that "the Jebusites dwell with the people of Judah at Jerusalem to this day" (Judges 1:21, which says the same about Benjamin). Historical accounts of Jerusalem do not answer all questions, but there is unanimous agreement that David captured the city (which came at the time to be called "Zion"). David established his capital there and made it the center of the nation's worship life (the cultic center) while it remained for Solomon, David's successor, to build the first and great temple, by centralizing the nation's religious life at Jerusalem, King David had accomplished two things: (1) in effect, he separated the religion of Israel from local, pagan influence, which tended to renew, purify, and reinvigorate it,

12 THE CHURCH IN PERSPECTIVE

and (2) he gave the nation not only a capable and good monarch but a *holy place*, thereby strengthening its sense of *national* identity. No one since the time of Moses had done so much to mold the twelve tribes into a united and proud—not to say prosperous—nation.

Except for his sin against Uriah (II Samuel 11), David was the quintessence of the good king. Under his enlightened rule, the nation prospered and religion was purified and strengthened. It did not fare so well under King Solomon.

Solomon came to the throne about 970 B.C. and ruled to 936. King Solomon is a legendary figure, more so even than his father David. He preferred the role of the extravagant eastern king to that of the servant king, which David had assumed. Reputed to have been very wise—which was said of all kings (I Kings 3:16ff is a legend commonly attributed to several ancient eastern kings)—he was actually anything but wise. His extravagances demoralized and divided permanently the kingdom he had inherited. He maintained a harem of as many as a thousand "wives," many of whom were foreigners. Although Solomon provided Israel with its great temple (I Kings 5-8), he allowed his foreign wives to practice their pagan religious rites in the midst of the people of Israel—he even built shrines for them. This was extremely expensive and required that he enslave his people to obtain laborers. His policies undermined seriously the worship of Yahweh, which had been carefully established. The discontent to which Solomon's excesses gave birth exploded into rebellion at his death. The northernmost ten of the twelve tribes of Israel followed Jeroboam and the two southern ones, Rehoboam. Thus, the united kingdom came to an end, dissolving into the kingdoms of Isreal in the North and Judah in the South. Jeroboam led this rebellion and followed it with the apostate worship of golden bulls.

After the breakup of the united kingdom, the Kingdom of Israel reverted to the pagan worship of Yahweh, centered in Jerusalem. From Jeroboam's revolt in the middle of the eighth century B.C. down to the eventual defeat and deportation of the northern kingdom in 722 B.C. by Assyrians under Sargon II (from which the people later returned), the northern kingdom fared badly and its religious life deteriorated seriously. But just as healing takes place only in the midst of hurt, and goodness takes meaning from the evil set against it, the deterioration of religion in Israel gave birth to a religious development of staggering importance, the appearance of the prophets.

The Prophetic Period

The story of the northern Kingdom of Israel is told by First Isaiah, Amos, Hosea, and Micah. The religious situation in Judah was the particular concern of Zephaniah, Jeremiah, Ezekiel, Nahum, and Habakkuk.

Although the Kingdom of Judah survived better and longer than did Israel, it too was the victim of conquest. In 586 B.C., the Kingdom of Judah was conquered by Nebuchadnezzar, king of the Babylonian Empire. Its people were deported in what history knows as the Babylonian Captivity of the Jews, about which some of the Psalms speak so beautifully (Psalms 4, 87, 137). The fall of Judah involved the seige of Jerusalem (Jeremiah 37 and 38).

Despite the advantage of having access to the Temple in Jerusalem, religious life in Judah did not, on the whole, fare much better than in the North, for a small state strategically located was not likely to maintain its independence for very long. In the early seventh century B.C., Judah came under Assyrian domination and, as a vassal state, had to pay homage to the gods of its Assyrian overlords. The religious climate changed radically at that time: pagan fertility cults appeared. Sacred prostitution was permitted even at the Temple (II Kings 21:7, Zephaniah 1:4f); fortune telling and the practice of mediums invoking the dead began, and human sacrifice reappeared. This was the religious climate in which the prophets lived and against which they preached, with immense effect.

In general, the prophets explained the defeats and humiliation of the Chosen People as punishment for sin and they formalized a future hope, if not for all in the nation, at least for the *Loyal Remnant* (Isaiah 11:11; in later prophecies, this was broadened to include all people).

Josiah's Reform

Prophecy, like every stage of Israel's development, came to an end, however, and, ironically, it was a sweeping religious reform that ended it. By calling upon the nation to repent, and promising deliverance if it did so, the prophets laid the groundwork for the reform that came in the reign of King Josiah of Judah in 605 B.C. There, during some restoration work on the Temple, was found a copy of the Law, which may have been brought from the Northern Kingdom at the time of its fall. The times called for religious reform because the nation's life had become blatantly apostate and openly pagan. The reform took the shape of rededication of the nation to the word of the Law. This rededication was a passionate, literalistic, slavish obedience to the letter of the Law, given on Sinai. The reform movement led away from prophecy to legal and formal observance. This had the effect of purifying Israel's religion of foreign influences and bringing to an end the need for the ministry of the prophets. The Law had need of priests and sacrifices, not of prophets. The reform, therefore, established a clergy monopoly in Jerusalem.[1] The transition from prophetic to legalistic religion was gradual, to be sure, but the elevation of the Law was the direct outcome of Josiah's reform and, by later postexilic times, was the characteristic principle around which the religion of Yahweh came to be organized. Initially, the reform was healthy but in time it became spiritually stultifying as the idea of divine blessing secured by compliance to the letter of the Law gained acceptance.

The evolution of the characteristic form of Israel's religious response to Yahweh is important to the student of Christianity.

---

1. John Bright, *The History of Israel* [Philadelphia, 1952).

The faith that finds expression in pre-Christian Israel was not stable and consistent over the centuries. Beginning with monolatry, it shifted in emphasis on Law, prophecy, reassertion of the Law, and the growth of a powerful priest class. The priestly form typified the closing centuries of the pre-Christian era. The legalism of Israel's faith grew as the Law began to be clarified and codified, a tendency that went on until, as the close of the Old Testaments Age, the Hebrew was able to identify some six hundred or more commandments in the Scriptures alone (to say nothing of developing a Rabbinic tradition of still more commandments). Through the remainder of the Old Testament period, Israel remained a subject nation passing from the rule of one powerful nation to another (Assyria, Babylon, Media, Persia, Egypt, and finally Rome).

The Advent of Christ

Into this world of massive political, social, and cultural change was born the Messiah, our Lord Jesus Christ. This was the world some eighty generations ago.

Little is known about the daily affairs of Christ's life. We know he was a layman of the common class, a member of the Amaharitz, or peasantry. He lived some thirty-three years, and for thirty of them almost nothing about him is known. His ministry was but three years long.

When he began his ministry, he gathered a wide following from among the amaharitz, the uneducated people of the land. Simply put, he took the thousands of laws the Hebrews were obliged to follow and claimed that they boiled down to a double principle, which needed constant application: if a person really cares about God, and if he cares about his fellow men as much as he does about himself, he will offend neither God not man."This is the Law and the prophets." All of prophecy and all of the 2,500 or more commandments of the Law turn on this single twofold principle.

16 THE CHURCH IN PERSPECTIVE

Among Jesus' followers, an inner group of twelve emerged, they whom Christ sent out in his name. They were called Apostles (from the Greek word meaning "those sent"). They were not the only apostles (there were over seventy according to St. Luke 10:1, 17, but the twelve were, with St. Paul, the "chief apostles." Our clergy's commission, or ordination, dates back to Christ's commissioning of these Apostles.

Jesus and his apostles were Jews, and the Church as it existed in its first years was Jewish, even in its customs (see Acts 2:46, 3:1, for example). The only difference in worship was that the Christians celebrated the Eucharist or Holy Communion together in their houses, in addition to their normal Jewish observances. The breaking of bread at Holy Communion is the only service instituted by Christ himself.

As long as the Christian Church was Jewish, there was no problem about Holy Communion, but when Christianity spread among the Gentiles under the missionary work of St. Paul, a problem arose. The Law forbade Jews to have any table fellowship with Gentiles, and this meant that if Jewish Christians continued to try to be good Jews, they could not have fellowship with Gentile Christians. They could not make Eucharist together, in other words. Acts 15 describes the first council of bishops held by the church. It was this council, held in A.D. 49 at Jerusalem and presided over by St. James, the Lord's brother, that worked out a compromise. The decision of the Apostles was that St. Paul's ministry to the Gentiles (non-Jews) would continue, and that Gentiles would not be required to become *Jewish* Christians (keeping the whole Law) but would be required only to "abstain from [worship of] idols, from unchastity, and from what is strangled and from blood" (Acts 15:20). Thus, the way was opened by St. Paul's efforts, with a majority of the Apostles agreeing, that Christianity would *not* exclude non-Jews. It was to be inclusive (catholic) of all men, not a minor sect within Judaism.

Once this matter was settled, St. Paul resumed his missionary activities and continued in that work until his death—probably as a martyr—in Rome about A.D. 64. It was he who first introduced Christianity into Europe, so far as we know, and he who wrote the earliest of the New Testament, epistles, or letters. Owing to the amenities of one great civilization—an official language, trade and mails,—Christianity spread rapidly throughout the Roman Empire despite its illegal status. Christians were in conflict with the Roman government because, in the totalitarian Roman Empire, religion was a department of the state. Allegiance to the state religion was the proof of allegiance to the state itself and, because Christians were forbidden by the First Commandment to have more than one God, they came into conflict with the state, whose emperor was worshiped as a god. This resulted in Christians in the Roman Empire being subjected to several bloody persecutions. They were law abiding and undoubtedly made good citizens, but their refusal to bow down and worship the emperor made them live under the constant threat of death. Some of the books of the New Testament reflect the danger of persecution (I Corinthians; Galatians). Moreover, since those not baptized were excluded from Christian worship, the Church was suspect as a secret society.

Toward the end of the first century, two significant, directly related developments took place: the Apostles grew old and began to die and the New Testament was written. Before that time, Christians expected Christ's return and the end of the world in their own lifetime. The Apostles had known and lived with the Lord, and there seemed no reason to preserve written records of what occurred or of what our Lord had taught. As Christianity spread, however, and as the aged Apostles (by now settled down in geographical centers which they supervised and over which they were *episcopoi* began to die, the need for written records grew more urgent. St. Paul had earlier developed the habit of writing to local churches he had founded or which he intended to visit, and the New Testament story had thus begun to be written. Now, several decades after Christ's departure, the gospels and remaining books were composed. The gospels were written as accounts of events carried in the memory for many, many years, and it is little short of amazing how superficial the discrepancies among them are!

But another task confronted the apostolic Church, which was to provide for a succession of leaders. This was done without fanfare or debate because the Church had already met the need for "commissioning" or ordaining new ministers. It had done so first in the case of St. Matthias, who was chosen by lot to replace Judas Iscariot, the suicidal betrayer of Christ. It had then instituted and ordained an order of deacons of whom St. Stephen, the first Christian martyr, was one. These were many other forms of ministry, and St. Paul names some in I Corinthians 12 (for example, leaders, prophets, and teachers) and in I Timothy 5 (widows), but the apostolic faith was mediated through a ministry of bishops (or apostles who supervised a given area), elders (priests), and deacons. Whether the distinction between bishops and priests (or apostles and presbyters) was as sharp and different as we know it today is somewhat questionable, but the appropriate functions were unquestionably carried on. By the end of the first century, the threefold ministry of bishops, presbyters (priests), and deacons had been accepted everywhere as the normal ministry by which the Church's apostolic witness would be directed through the generations to come. This is Apostolic Succession.

Life in the Church during the first three centuries was, as we have seen, distressed by persecutions (which were occasional and more or less local) and the fear of them (which was constant and general). In the fourth century, this all changed. As the third century drew to a close, the Roman emperor Diocletian divided the Empire in two for better administration, the capitals being Rome and Constantinople. Instead of working in favor of better administration, however, this made rivals of the eastern and western emperors. The rivalry continued until A.D. 312, when it ended with the victory of Constantine, who defeated five rival "emperors" and restored a reunified Roman Empire to a single ruler. In the civil strife that accompanied his rise to power, most of Constantine's rivals showed themselves to be opponents and persecutors of the Christians. Constantine favored the Christians, possibly to enlist their support, and in 313, as Emperor of the East and West, legalized Christianity by his famous Edict of Milan. Shortly thereafter, he himself became a Christian. This is an immensely important development, because it had a double significance that changed radically the tone of Christian life: (1) it ended the threat of persecution, the need for secrecy, and the need for the careful screening and testing of would-be converts and (2) it set the climate in which monasticism appeared.

In the ancient world, it was traditional for the whole citizenry of a nation to accept, officially at least, the emperor's religion as their own. Thus, when Constantine became a Christian, his followers felt they should do likewise, which resulted in a tremendous influx into the Church of people not *really* converted, but only joining it because it was the official national religion. Empires did not admit more than one religion in those days, and it was inconceivable to people of that time that there could be such a thing as a pluralistic society—a society like ours, with religious freedom. When Constantine made Christianity his religion, he made it the religion of the whole Roman Empire. The effect of this upon Christian discipline was devastating. Many of the new converts were at best lukewarm, and for Christians who had belonged to the Church in the resent years of persecution, many of whom had seen loved ones put to death by those who now sought to be baptized and admitted into the Christian Church, the Roman converts were very difficult to accept. The reaction of devout Christians of long standing to the slackened discipline they saw was an effort to correct this evil. They wanted to protest against the erosion of the Church's standards and perhaps also to find some ultimate expression of commitment to Christ in a world in which martyrdom was no longer probable. They found the outlet they needed in monasticism.

The history of monasticism is long and complicated. Apparently, its appearance within the Christian faith is best linked with St. Pacomius, whom we believe to have been the first Christian monk. At first, to be a monk was to be a hermit, because all monks lived alone. The idea of a monastic *community* is one of the particular contributions of St. Benedict (sixth century—died 543), often called the father of Western Monasticism, who founded the famous monastery of Monte Cassino, which was destroyed in World War II and only recently restored.

The Faith Once Delivered Unto the Saints

Everyone who thinks anything at all about God is some kind of theologian. Not all theologians are good ones. Bad theology has never been hard to find, and it is easy to demonstrate that most bad theology (or thought about God) has some of its roots in a pagan belief or superstition. The chapters on doctrine discuss the content of the classical false teachings. Here we will concern ourselves with the church's response to them.

Most of the heresies the Church faced were in the general area of *Christology*—having to do with belief in or about Jesus Christ. Moreover, most of these false teachings tended to accept Christ's divinity and deny his full humanity. The denials as we shall see, took many different forms. In rebuttal to these false teachings, the Church carefully defined what the truth was, and a body of Christian theology came into being. Typically, the means of determining the truth in matters of faith was the General or Ecumenical Council—a council to which all Christian bishops came. There have been only four such councils. Others, though claiming to be ecumenical, have been in fact denominational and represented the bishops of only one communion. These later councils are ecumenical in the sense that the bishops attending them, though members of one denomination, come from all over the world, but that is not the historic meaning of the word ecumenical.

The first council met at Nicea in Asia Minor in A.D. 325, called by the Emperor Constantine. The issue it faced was Christ's equality with God. The orthodox position assumed equality. The opposing position, led by Arius, denied equality on the ground that a son is dependent on the father for his being born and therefore is of lesser dignity. The issue was really whether or not Christ was "of one substance with the Father" and therefore actually God himself "in the flesh." The council, though bitter in argument, finally settled on the statement we have in our creed:"...of one substance with the Father" and, therefore, so far as his divinity is concerned, the same as the Father.

As time went on, it became clear that the Council of Nicea had not settled fully the Arian heresy, or *Arianism*, so in 381 another general council was convened in Constantinople. This council actually settled the Arian controversy and its creedal statement is, with but one brief ninth century addition, the Nicene Creed we use today. The Council of Constantinople also dealt with two other heresies. *Macedonianism* (which taught, in effect, that Christ had no human spirit and in Jesus, what corresponds to the spirit in man was God).

Of all the doctrines, or teachings, that the early Church condemned, none has recurred more frequently or been circulated more widely than *Nestorianism*. Nestorianism was the belief that Christ was not only human in every sense that we are, but that his relationship with God is *no different from ours*, except that he possessed more of the Holy Ghost than has any other man. According to Nestorianism, Christ's relationship with God differed from ours only in *degree*, not in *kind*. The Nestorian controversy actually focused on another question, whether or not the Virgin Mary deserved the title "Mother of God." Nestorius was a monk and a very sophisticated theologian who lived in Antioch in the fifth century. His chaplain fired the opening gun, opposing the term "Mother of God" on the grounds that it implied an Appollinarian view of Christ. The controversy led directly to the calling of a third general council at Ephesus in the year 431.

From the point of view of Church history, the fourth general council was the most important. It was the Council of Chalcedon held in A.D. 451. Nestorianism was especially associated with Antioch, an ancient center of theological study. Another theological center, however, was Alexandria in Egypt, where developed the heresy which led to the fourth general council, *Monophysitism* ("one-nature-ism"). The theologians of Alexandria leaned so far in opposition to Nestorianism (Christ was a man linked to God only by possession of Spirit) that they fell into the opposite error of saying that Christ was so intimately related to God that his human nature was mixed with the divine nature of God. The theological problem here is that if one nature has a mixture of divine and human natures it is fully neither. To believe this about our Lord is to believe that he is neither fully human nor fully divine, but *half* human and *half* divine. By its condemnation of Monophysitism the Council of Chalcedon further defined the historic Christian faith. This is the important function of the general council in the church's historic life. From early times, it came to be the agency for determining matters of faith. Since it was a council of bishops, it was the means whereby the Church functioned *episcopally* (from the Greek word, *episcopos*, meaning supervisor or bishop) in its belief and practice. At the height of the Monophysite controversy, Pope Leo I wrote a letter in which he defined what was believed in the Western Church about Christ's human and divine natures, and the Council of Chalcedon accepted that letter, which is called The Tome of Leo. The council accepted the pope's letter because it accurately described the faith of the Church in the West, not because, as later popes have claimed, the pope alone has the right to define what is true in matters of faith and morality.

The Middle Ages

By the end of the fifth century, the twofold principle of episcopal government and conciliar authority (or the authority of a general council of bishops) had been established by precedent and by consent. Another immensely important fact had also been established: the importance in Western Christendom of the See of Rome. In the life of the early Church, there were several important centers. From them, each of which claimed to have apostolic origin, bishops ruled over vast areas of the known world. Four of these ancient patriarchates, as they are called, lay in the East. Only Rome was in the West. Of the five—Rome, Antioch, Alexandria, Constantinople, and Jerusalem—only Rome could lay claim to "Double apostolic foundation," for by tradition both St. Peter and St. Paul had labored and been martyred there. These two factors are significant in accounting for the ascendancy of Rome's power and prestige in the Western Church.

Another factor in the rise of the papacy, is the role of the emperor in the life of the Church (the relationship of Church and State). Constantine, the emperor who had legalized the Christian Church and brought its persecution to an end, moved the capital of the empire to Constantinople. This meant that in the West there was no higher ranking dignitary than the pope, and his prestige was enormously enhanced by the pre-eminence of Rome. The practice of the four Eastern patriarchs of appealing their disputes to Rome had dignity because Rome was the only Western patriarchate and was regarded as a disinterested party qualified reasonably to arbitrate theological disputes. By the fifth century A.D., quarrelling Eastern patriarchs were making Rome not just arbiter of differences but *definer of the faith* as well. This was the background against which the papal claims of primacy and authority would later be made, and these events took on new meaning in the face of the fall of Rome in the closing decades of the fifth century.

The fifth century saw hordes of Germanic invaders pour into

Italy, France, Spain, and North Africa. As the highest authority in the ancient capital of Rome, and with a constituency of Catholics all over Europe, the pope alone could withstand the invaders. Thus, the papacy became a symbol of stability in the midst of a critical and massive social change that brought with it the Dark Ages. Because Pope Leo I had twice persuaded the invaders not to sack Rome, he was regarded by Romans, pagans and Christians alike, as their protector. Later, when the pagan invaders began to convert to Christianity, even they naturally looked to Rome and the pope as arbiter in disputes with the native Catholic population. Thus, out of the debris of the Roman Empire, the pope emerged as the undisputed religious and secular leader in the Western world.

The history of the Middle Ages is written to a great extent in terms of the church-state relationship. Gradually, there evolved distinct areas of responsibility between the Church and the secular ruler; and by the late ninth century, a sort of accommodation had been reached between them. The Holy Roman Emperor ruled the state; the pope ruled the Church. The pope was guardian of the faith and kept the Church loyal to the emperor. In exchange for this loyalty, the emperor provided munificent funds for the church-state relationship through the remainder of the Middle Ages in the Western Church.

No medieval event was more significant in shaping the present-day Church than the breach that occurred between the East and the West in the eleventh century. East and West have never been close either in outlook or sensitivities, and the course of their relationship has never run smoothly. In the ninth century, a breach developed between Rome and Constantinople. It involved, among other things, Constantinople's resentment of Rome's celibacy requirements for clergy, separation of baptism and confirmation, and alteration of the Nicene Creed by the ninth century addition of the three words concerning the Holy Ghost, that "He proceedeth from the Father *and the Son*." Although the breach was healed temporarily, it opened again in the eleventh century and the East-West schism has lasted from 1054 to the present day. The historic Eastern Churches are Orthodox, and the historic Western, or Latin, are now either Roman or Reformed. The Middle Ages moved to a close with the Christian world tragically divided in two and the Church in the West sadly weakened from within by centuries of corruption. Chief among the abuses upon which corruption in the Church fed was the sale of positions in the ministry (simony). The Practice had virtually placed the Church in the hands of incompetent and unscrupulous men. In an effort to reform the Church, the emperor Henry III (1017-1056) took a dominant role in Church political disputes, thus establishing a precedent for the emperor's being, in a sense, superior to the pope. This spawned a battle between the Church and State as to which would invest new bishops with their authority, which is called the Investiture Controversy. Pope Gregory VII resolved the controversy in the opening decade of the twelfth century by a judicious compromise in which a new bishop received the staff and ring, symbolizing his pastoral authority, from the Church and the symbols of temporal authority, as a feudal noble, from the emperor. The importance of the Investiture Compromise to the rise of papal power is immense, for it was a compromise on the emperor's side and was tantamount to an admission that the popes authority was *equal* to, though *different* from, that of the emperor. Although the Crusades, which were fought at this time, are better remembered than the Investiture Compromise, the latter was by far the more significant in shaping the Church as it exists today. Moreover, it established the papacy in a position from which it could patronize the efforts and reap the benefits of the Renaissance.

The Renaissance Church

At the close of the Middle Ages, a rebirth of the religious life occurred. Between the eleventh and thirteenth centuries, several religious orders appeared. The Carthusians, Cistercians, Trappists, and Franciscans had joined the older orders, the Benedictines, the Augustinians, and the Dominicans. It is on the work of a Dominican monk, St. Thomas Aquinas, that "Scholastic Theology" (the body of theological thought inherited, not from the early church, but from the Middle Ages. A.D. 500-1500) is largely based. He also composed poems and hymns, and parts of four of his hymns appear in our present hymnal. His most famous writing was the huge *Summa Theologica*, which had the double significance of stabilizing the faith by codifying it and of stultifying the Church's future theological development to the present century. Even today, most of the conservative theology of the Roman Communion is that of St. Thomas Aquinas, substantially unaltered since the thirteenth century.

The fourteenth and fifteenth centuries are notable for the Papal Schism. It began in 1305 when Pope Clement V, a Frenchman, decided to move the papal see to Avignon in France. His successor, Pope John XXII, remained in Avignon, but Gregory XI, next in line, was persuaded by St. Catherine of Siena, in 1377, to return the papacy to Rome. This seventy-two year interlude is called "The Babylonian Captivity of the Papacy." When Gregory XI died, the people of Rome brought enormous pressure to bear on the cardinals to elect a Roman, reasoning that a Roman pope would keep the papacy in Italy. Not wanting to be intimidated, the cardinals refused to have a Roman but did select an Italian. He was Urban VI, a poor choice and a poor strategist as well, who turned on his cardinals and incited rebellion among them. The cardinals declared his election invalid and chose a new pope, another Frenchman, Clement VIII. The new pope forthwith moved the papacy back to Avignon. Two men in two places each claiming to be the legitimate pope was an impossible situation that sundered the Church. In 1409, a council was convened in Pisa to deal with it. It declared both popes deposed and elected a new one, John XXIII (who reigned 1410-1415). This "Pisan Pope" was supported by England, France, and certain areas in Germany and Italy, so the Church now had three popes claiming to be the legitimate Vicar of Christ.

This John XXIII, to whom the situation was perhaps most intolerable, called another council to solve it, the Council of Constance, which met in 1414. By removing these three rival claimants to the papacy, the Church reasserted the ancient principle of conciliar authority developed in the fourth and fifth centuries: that a council is superior to a pope and historically the Church is rightly Episcopal, not papal. The reassertion of this principle was of importance at the Reformation and is an issue between conservatives and liberals in modern Roman Catholicism. In spite of this conciliar challenge to papal domination, however, the pope retained his power undiminished. A later council, the Council of Florence, which met in 1439, strengthened the pope's hands by forbidding future appeals to General Councils. This action, however, made the Catholic Church indisputably papal, not Episcopal.

The fifteenth and sixteenth centuries were bad times for the Church, times in which the discontent was bred that was to burst forth during the Reformation. Popes engaged in warfare to enhance their secular prerogatives; they practiced nepotism, placing relatives in positions of power, honor, and wealth. The sales of indulgences and of masses and other sacraments became commonplace. The church gradually sank into a mire of corruption.

The Background of the Reformation

The story of the Reformation is such a complex of diverse factors that anything less than an exhaustive study will give one a foreshortened and inadequate perspective of it. At the risk of oversimplification, however, four historic developments can be cited as the conditions that set the climate for the Reformation.

The first of these was the breakup of feudalism. During the

Middle Ages, society was organized on a class or caste basis rather than by nations. At the top of the class structure was the local lord or king. He ruled a small area, which varied in size according to his success in warfare against neighboring nobles. Since people thought of themselves in terms of their social class, and their primary kinship or loyalty was felt toward members of their own social class, they felt no special loyalty to the general population of a particular geographical section or nation. This is the key to understanding feudal society. Nobles felt themselves more closely related to other nobles than to the peasants over whom they ruled.

Another factor militating against geographical loyalties was the conditions of travel. Merchants, for example, became interdependent, and as cooperation among them seemed to be in their best interests, they developed some ground for loyalty based on common interests. Gradually, they came to constitute a social class, which extended across vast areas of Europe without ties to any local region. In like manner, scholars wandered freely between centers of learning and their travels tended to leave them without local ties. Perhaps the clergy were the most remote of all from the local loyalties, not only because they traveled a great deal, but also because, just as foreign diplomats are free from prosecution under alien laws today, the clergy were then beyond the jurisdiction of secular courts, being subject only to church law. Their "diplomatic immunity" was widely resented.

During the Middle Ages, Europe had one official language—Latin—the language of the Western Church. Although local tongues existed, there was not the regional or geographical demarcation of languages that we are accustomed to—at least not before the thirteenth century. Modern national languages date from about that time coincident with the formation of nations. Through most of the Middle Ages, people did not think of themselves as English, French, or Italian, etc. After the thirteenth century, people gradually began to have some sense of national identity; with the advent of nations and national languages, they began to have national, rather than feudal, loyalties. In feudal society, there were only three classes: royalty, religious, and peasants.

The second factor, along with the breakup of feudalism, which helped make possible the Reformation, was the appearance of a middle class. The middle class was composed of merchants and craftsmen, whose economic activity gradually brought them considerable political power—power they used to hasten the end of the feudal system with its incessant wars. The merchants wanted peace and stability in which to ply their trade, and they recognized that strong central governments furthered the political stability necessary for economic prosperity. Throughout the fourteenth and fifteenth centuries, the merchants grew in power by consolidating their enterprises in towns and cities. Thus began the great trend of urbanization, which prevails today. As they organized according to their economic interests in craft guilds, they began the trend toward labor unions, which are now almost universal.

The mercantile activity that made possible the emergence of the middle class gave birth to new interest in culture. The same traders who brought wealth into Europe from the East, and whose interests influenced the growth of towns and national governments, also captured the imagination of Europe with the riches of Greek culture. Suddenly, the study of Greek language and art came into vogue, and the flood gates of classical Greek sophistication in philosophy, politics, and literature opened upon an intellectually parched Europe. The Renaissance had begun!

The Renaissance was a period of incredible productivity. It was the age of the masters, an age that gave the world of genius of Botticelli, da Vinci, Raphael, Michelangelo, Cellini, and others. Moreover, there came with the Renaissance inventions that had far-reaching significance, among which were gunpowder and printing with movable type. Exploration was extending human dominion over the earth with the discoveries of Columbus, Vasco da Gama, and Prince Henry the Navigator. The work of Copernicus in the sixteenth century and of Galileo in the seventeenth measurably extended knowledge of the universe; together the discoveries of the Renaissance unraveled much of life's mystery, relieved much of its misery, and made life more comfortable, secure, and interesting. As life became more pleasant the need for a future heavenly home appeared less urgent; people became more detached from, as well as critical of, the Church. Increasingly, the Church and the world came into conflict.

The Church's response to the Renaissance was to patronize and encourage it and, up to a point, the Renaissance served the Church well. Gradually, however, conflict developed on many fronts. As nations were formed, their sovereignty was challenged by the clergy's legal immunity from prosecution. As merchants became aware of their power, they saw the concentrated wealth of the Church as a force to be reckoned with and its high taxes as a drain upon local economies. New learning exposed serious faults in the Church's practice and profession. The total effect of the Renaissance was the widespread disillusionment of the laity. This disenchantment with the Church's pomp, power and prerogatives coincided with the development of new careers, in politics, art, literature, and scholarship, which had not existed before. In the Middle Ages, the Church was but one of many options open to the individual. As most of the new professions concerned themselves with human welfare and happiness rather that upon God's glory, secularism was born.

The Reformation and Its Aftermath

In the fifteenth and sixteenth centuries, in addition to being faced with external conflict, the Western Church was split asunder with internal strife. In these centuries, the moral tone of the Church reached its nadir. Throughout Europe, the pope was recognized as the leader of the Church. The popes were usually Italian princes and, as such, sought to expand the territory of the Papal States. They engaged in extravagances that staggered the imagination and paid for them by selling church positions and offices, by levying papal taxes, by selling pardons and dispensations (indulgences), masses, and other sacraments.

Before the storm of the Reformation broke, efforts were made by loyal church members to bring about reform. These would-be reformers stood on the shoulders of those Renaissance scholars whose work was the translating of Scripture and the researching of old documents. They were scholars loyal to the Church. They believed, however, that ignorance had made possible the corrupt morals they saw in the Church, and they were dedicated foes of that pernicious ignorance. Called "The Humanists" because of their faith in the New Learning, or the "Catholic Reformers" because they tried to change the Church from within, their leaders were Desiderius Erasmus, John Colet, and Thomas More. The story of their noble efforts is fascinating reading. The significance of the efforts of these three resides in their failure. They demonstrated by it that the Church under *absolute* papal domination could not be reformed from within, and their failure had the effect of justifying the Reformation.

The Reformation has two parts, generally referred to as if they were two separate Reformations, the Continental Reformation and the English Reformation. The Reformation began on the Continent in 1517, when Martin Luther posted his "95 theses." Luther was a very sensitive, emotional man who had never been entirely in agreement with Western Catholicism, and who came into open disagreement with it after his famous conversion experience. His conversion was profoundly affecting, and it settled his conviction that human beings are saved only by faith—faith that God will save them for Christ's sake, the Lord having offered himself for all who believe. Luther believed in "justification by faith" exclusively, insisting that works were without any value in shaping one's eternal destiny. Another of Luther's beliefs was "the priesthood of all believers."

Like his own view on justification, the orthodoxy of his teaching depended on how it was understood. Both ideas contained essential truths, and both can readily be expressed in ways consistent with the Church's ancient apostolic faith. Luther had no intention of breaking with the Church, but he had earned the warm hatred of the Dominican Order by bitterly opposing the sale of indulgences, with which the Dominicans were linked. That was his downfall. One Dominican friar, Johann Mayer Eck, opposed Luther in debate at Leipzig in 1519. Eck was a brilliant debater and, having trapped Luther into challenging the pope's authority to grant indulgences, he forced Luther to assert his conviction that a general council has final authority in doctrine and not the pope. Eck then led Luther to admit that he, Luther, accepted the teachings of John Hus. The Council of Constance, recognized by all as a general council, had condemned these teachings, and Luther had been made to contradict himself in public debate. In effect, he rejected papal *and* conciliar authority. His only recourse was to assert that authority in doctrine could consist only of the Scriptures *as each man's conscience understood them*. The authority of individual conscience is the cornerstone upon which Protestantism was built.

Luther went on to make other changes in doctrine and practice: services in German, the giving of the chalice at Communion to the laity, the condemnation of monasticism, allowing clergy to marry, as he himself did, forbidding the invocation of saints, belief in purgatory, and in transubstantiation (the physical changing of bread and wine into the Body and Blood of Christ in the Eucharist).

Although the continental Reformation began with Luther, it did not end with him. The Anabaptists emerged at this time as a reform element that went further than Luther. They took their name from being "baptized again," for they rejected the validity of infant baptism and regarded immersion as the only valid means of baptism. They laid this stress on baptism because it expressed to their minds the conscious conversion experience of the responsible adult. Their other "reforms" included a congregational structure based upon a rejection of Holy Orders as a ministry distinct from that of the laity and various liturgical reforms that would stem inevitably from such a viewpoint. As to doctrinal authority, they superseded Luther's dictum of Holy Scripture interpreted by individual conscience with a belief in *direct personal revelation independent of Scripture*. Luther could perhaps have been reconciled with them except for this last point. In response to their individualism, Luther took the position, which is native to the Anglican genius as well, that nothing which is not contained in the Scriptures can be taught as necessary to salvation. The Anabaptists, originally located in Germany, were forebears of the Mennonites, named after their leader Menno Simons, and of the Baptists.

In Switzerland, the Reformation found leadership in the person of Huldreich Zwingli. In many ways, like the German Lutherans, Zwingli's followers went further than Luther in restating the theology of the Eucharist. They not only rejected transubstantiation, they denied that Christ was really present (Real Presence) in any sense in the mass. This is called "memorialism" as opposed to "transubstantiation." In the course of time, they were absorbed by the Calvinists, who formed still another major Reformation group.

John Calvin was a French lawyer and, although in the church's employ, a layman. He became an advocate of reform and was so urgent in his effort to bring it about that he finally had to flee for safety. Going first to Basel and later to Geneva, he published his famous book, *The Institutes*. It is virtually a catalog of Protestant Reformation theology and is something of a summa," or compendium, on the subject. Calvin agreed with Luther on the issue of justification by faith only, apart from works, but he went a good deal further. He taught that by virtue of Adam's disobedience all people were totally depraved; they were incapable of doing any good and deserved damnation. Christ paid the ransom that freed human beings from Satan's power, but he paid only for those whom

God means to save, not for all. God, according to the Calvinist view, does *not* intend that *all* people will be saved. He has predestined some for salvation and some to damnation. This is the doctrine of double predestination: *nothing* anyone does can change these eternal decrees. The elect are saved; all others are lost. Christ will save only *some*, by paying ransom for them to the Devil. Calvin's system did not exclude good works entirely, however, for he regarded them a proof that one was a member of the group elected to salvation.

Calvin was a lawyer through and through, and to his mind the Scriptures, which were the source of authority for doctrine, constituted a law book, which was to be followed literally. The doctrine of double predestination reflects his legalistic approach to religion. It is so obviously crude that today even most Calvinists reject it.

Calvin made many changes in the Church's life, but none was more significant than that which resulted from his belief about bishops. He thought bishops were really presbyters, so he eliminated the episcopal rank and made his church presbyterial (hence the name Presbyterian to describe Calvinist churches today). He agreed with Luther in rejecting the doctrine of transubstantiation, and he tried to reconcile the notion of the real presence in the Eucharist, which was Luther's conviction, to Zwingli's memorialism. which denied and real presence of Christ. He did it by saying that Christ's presence in the Communion is in the heart of the faithful. The theological name for this doctrine is "receptionism." He derived this teaching from I Corinthians 11:29: "He that eats and drinks unworthily, eats and drinks to his own damnation, not discerning the Lord's Body." He rid his segment of the Church of its religios (monastic) orders, and he carried the idea of the general priesthood of the Church to the extreme of eliminating priests as such, as well as bishops. He had, therefore, as distinct from Episcopalianism, Presbyterianism, and Papalism, a *Congregationalism*. These are four different kinds of Church government.

In England, the Reformation centered on the person of Henry

VIII who, however deficient in virtue he may have been in his private life, was an outstandingly capable theologian. Enlightened Roman Catholics acknowledge Henry VIII's theological acumen for, when Martin Luther produced his book attacking the sacramental practice of the Church, *The Babylonian Captivity of the Church*, Henry VIII wrote the Church's rebuttal to it, *Assertion of the Seven Sacraments*. It was so good the pope conferred on Henry VIII the title every English king or queen bears to this day, "Defender of the Faith."

The breach with Rome was precipitated by Henry's desire to be free from Catherine of Aragon. He obtained that freedom not by securing a divorce (which was unthinkable to a good Catholic) but by obtaining an annulment on the grounds that prior to their marriage, Catherine had been his sister-in-law. Leviticus 18:16 forbids marriage with one's sister-in-law, and Henry simply claimed that the Pope, Julius II, who had granted a dispensation for the marriage, had no right to set aside the explicit teaching of Holy Scripture. In 1531-34, Henry brought about, by successive steps, changes that would establish him as head of the Church if a breach with the Pope came. In 1534 he was declared by Parliament the Supreme Head of the Church of England, "so far as the Law of Christ doth allow."

Unlike Thomas Cranmer, his Archbishop of Canterbury, a reformed churchman and author of the first *Book of Common Prayer*, Henry VIII was a devout Catholic. Although he challenged the right of the Pope to any ecclesiastical jurisdiction in England, he did not alter the substance of the faith. The doing away with monastaries was his only departure from Catholic practice, although later he did bring about other reforms, such as having the Bible translated into English. He retained belief in transubstantiation, Communion with worshipers receiving the host only and not the chalice, clerical celibacy, private masses, and auricular confession (confession to God *through* the person of a priest).

Under Edward VI, a child king, England was governed by the Duke of Northumberland. He made reforms allowing communion in both kinds and clergy marriages, and had his opponents arrested. Under the regency of the Duke of Northumberland, Cranmer, in 1549, wrote the first *Book of Common Prayer* (see section on Liturgy). In 1552, a second edition of the *Book of Common Prayer*, more Protestant in substance, was issued but was never officially approved. It was replaced ten years later by the present, distinctly Catholic, edition.

In 1553, Mary Tudor became queen and, having had Cranmer arrested, returned England to the Church of Rome. At one point in his trial, Cranmer signed a retraction of his teachings; when he later repudiated the retraction, he was burned at the stake. As the fire rose around him, he thrust the right hand with which he had signed the retraction into the flame and saw it burn to a stump before the rest of his body perished. The bishops and clergy who would not accept papal domination fled to the Continent, where they came under the influence of leaders of the continental Reformation. These exiles returned to England during the reign of Elizabeth I, and the "Low Church," the evangelical tradition within Anglicanism, came with them. Those whose sensitivities and sympathies were Catholic made up the "High Church" tradition. Her persecution of Protestants earned for Mary Tudor the nickname "Bloody Mary." Although she accepted the authority of Pope Paul IV, Mary refused to restore to him the Church property confiscated by Henry VIII.

Elizabeth I ruled from 1558 to 1603. Under her influence, Anglicanism pursued a course between Protestant and Catholic extremes, assuming by this "middle road" (*via media*) much of the character with which it has entered the second half of the twentieth century. Elizabeth *did not* claim, as her father Henry VIII had done, to be Supreme Head of the Church. She instigated reforms by which she hoped to unite her Calvinist and Romanist subjects. The thirty-nine Articles of Religion, which are still bound into the back of the Prayer Book of the American Church, were originally issued under Elizabeth (see Chapter II). She filled episcopal vacancies with care and discretion.

Elizabeth found in the papacy a perennial enemy, however. It was the pope who established the Jesuits as missionaries to Protestant countries and who authorized the Roman Catholic English Bible (the Douai Version) as a tool to win back England. In 1590, Pope Pius V declared Elizabeth excommunicated and deposed and called on Roman Catholics in England to do away with her—(thereby making all Romanists in England suspects for treason.) The papacy supported unsuccessful plots to have Mary Stuart executed. Finally, Pope Sixtus V supported Philip II of Spain when Philip launched the Spanish Armada to conquer England. In the battle that ensued, England defeated the Spaniards, effectively ending Roman Catholic hopes for a military conquest of Britain.

The history of the Church of England did not proceed from the time Elizabeth I to that of Elizabeth II without some serious upheavals, of course. James I, who succeeded Elizabeth I, was the son of Mary Queen of Scots. James followed Elizabeth's policies, and to his patronage the world owes the incomparably beautiful King James Version of the Bible. He also "catholicized" the hitherto Calvinist Church of Scotland, thereby engendering enormous Scotish-Anglican enmity. If anything, his son, Charles I, intensified James's anti-Calvinist policies in England.

After Charles I had ruled for eleven years without summoning the predominantly Calvinist Parliament, the Calvinists revolted against him and sought Scottish assistance in the civil war they precipitated. In 1645, Oliver Cromwell's Parliamentary forces defeated the king, but the enemies of the defeated monarch were divided denominationally into Congregationalists, Baptists, and Presbyterians. Because of that division, no one group established a dominant national religion and, when the monarchy was reinstated under Charles II in 1660, the Church of England was restored. Although sympathetic to Roman Catholicism, Charles allowed the revision of the Prayer Book, the new edition of 1662 remains in use in the English Church to this day.

Although party conflict continued within the Church of England, the pattern of English church life was now established. Today, that pattern is facing the serious challenge to change or perish. The Church of England has faced this challenge before, most notably during the early eighteenth century, when Methodism was born among dissident Anglicans led by John and Charles Wesley. The followers of the Wesley Movement who chose to remain within the Church of England constituted a remarkable reforming influence and became members of the evangelical, or Low Church, party.

The Counter-Reformation

One of Newton's laws of physical processes is: "To every action there is an equal and opposite reaction." We might frame a valid law of church life by saying much the same thing. The reaction to the Reformation was the Counter-Reformation, a resurgence of vitality in the Roman Church. It was characterized by three developments: (1) the founding of the Society of Jesus, (2) the Inquisition, and (3) the Council of Trent (1545-63).

The Society of Jesus, whose members are called Jesuits, was founded by Ignatius Loyola in 1540. Its members add to the three usual monastic vows of poverty, chastity, and obedience a fourth, the vow of absolute obedience to the pope. Preparation for full membership involves fourteen years of intensely thorough training. Although the Jesuits have been dramatically successful in missionary work, their first service to the pope was the recovery of large areas of Germany and France from the ranks of Protestantism. They became so deeply involved in political intrigue in the eighteenth century, however, that the pope suspended the order from 1773 to 1814.

The Inquisition was an ecclesiastical court for uncovering heretics, which made notorious use of torture. It was first used in Europe during the thirteenth century, but died out everywhere outside of Spain during the fifteenth century.

Under Pope Paul III, it was reintroduced, with some restraint, into Europe. Under Paul IV in the sixteenth century, it went into wide use. The Franciscans and Dominicans were especially associated with the Inquisition. Among their victims was Galileo. The Inquisition, more than anything else, kept Protestantism out of Italy.

The Council of Trent fashioned post-Reformation Roman Catholicism and made modern Romanism, before the Second Vatican Council, a Reformation faith. Forced on the Pope by the Holy Roman emperor, Charles V of Germany, the Council was controlled by papalists and therefore prevented from declaring its authority superior to the popes. The first two sessions were the really important ones, and they accomplished eleven things:

(1) Declared Bible and tradition to be equal in authority (as opposed to Luther's position).
(2) Declared the Vulgate to be the Church's authorized Bible and forbade its interpretation by anyone not in holy orders (not a priest or bishop).
(3) Denied the Calvinist teaching regarding the total depravity of man.
(4) Denied Luther's declaration of justification by faith only.
(5) Denied Calvin's doctrine of double predestination.
(6) Defined the seven sacraments.
(7) Denied wholesale all Protestant pronouncements about the Eucharist and reasserted the doctrine of transubstantiation.
(8) Defined the sacraments of penance and unction.
(9) Prohibited sale of indulgences "for illegal gains."
(10) Required that diocesan seminaries be established.
(11) Decreed that those who were not Roman were not Christian.

The significance of the Council of Trent is that it gave rigid form to Roman Catholic thought and practice. It did to Roman Catholic practice what St. Thomas' *Summa Theologica* did to

Roman Catholic theology, giving it a rigid regularity. There followed from these developments, together with the Spanish revival of piety which gave the world St. Theresa, St. John of the Cross, St. Francis de Sales, St. Philip Neri, and St. Vincent de Paul, a revitalized, strict, hierarchical Romanism familiar down to the time of recent Pope John XXIII.

II. THE DEVELOPMENT OF CHRISTIAN THEOLOGY

There is a story analogous to the present religious situation which raises the question the world is asking the Church. Two explorers are walking through the jungle, and they suddenly come upon a clearing in which is a beautiful, well-kept garden. One explorer claims that a gardener produced this, but the other insists that there is no gardener and, like the jungle, the garden just *happened*. They decide to test the theory by pitching camp and standing guard, and after a few days they have observed no gardener. The skeptical explorer finally confronts his companion with this, but he is met with even bolder insistence. "There is a gardener," the believing explorer maintains, "and part of his greatness is that he is an invisible gardener." To test this theory, they put up an electric fence around the garden and patrolled it day and night with bloodhounds. After a few days, hearing no cries to indicate contact with the electric fence and no barking from the dogs to warn of an unseen presence, the skeptical explorer again confronts his friend with the conviction that there is no gardener. Again the believing explorer is insistent. "There is a gardener and he is not only invisible, he is intangible and insensitive to electric fences, and he comes and cares for the garden he loves." At this point the skeptic throws up his hands. "What," he asks, "is the difference between your invisible, intangible, insensitive gardener, or an *imaginary gardener—or no gardener at all?*"2

The parable confronts us with the question put to Christians today: "What is the difference between an invisible, intangible, unchangeable, eternally elusive God and an imaginary God, or no God at all?" Obviously, the answer is not easy, and the problem is complicated by the fact that *Christianity today is entering a third era.*

The first Christian era was the period between the years A.D. 1 and A.D. 313. This was an *eschatological era. Eschaton* means "the last things" and was the primary concern of Christianity in its early years. Christians expected the end of the world at any moment; therfore, their religious orientation was forward toward eternity. The only religious holidays universally observed by Christians in those centuries were Sunday and the Pascha a combination of Easter and the Ascension. These were understood to be celebrations of a future event, namely the completion of Christ's redemption and his heavenly reign. The about-face in the Church's primary religious orientation took place in the fourth century. In 313, the emperor Constantine legalized the Church and became a Christian. His subjects joined the Church by the thousands and nearly split the Church apart. As we have seen, with mass conversions came a breakdown in Church discipline and the infiltration of pagan ideas. One reaction to the influence of pagan thought was the development of orthodox theology. The reversal in the Church's primary religious orientation was the

---

2. This parable was originally told in a slightly different form by the British theologian Antony Flew and appeared in *New Essays in Philosophical Theology*, edited by Antony Flew and Alasdair MacIntyre (London, 1955), p.96.

The Development of Christian Theology 43

new concern, always present but previously not dominant, for tradition. Christians became aware of threats from within that would pervert and dilute "the faith once delivered unto the saints," and their concern to guard faithfully the Church's teaching tradition became a preoccupation. Accompanying this concern for tradition was a view that looked *backward into history*, a jealous preoccupation with apostolic tradition that was the mark or characteristic orientation of the Church down to our own day.

But now a new age is dawning, as an outgrowth of science, for as new knowledge brings nature increasingly under human control, it creates a world vastly different from the world of thought in which our traditional theology, or way of understanding God, took shape. Traditional theology began in a world in which life was pitifully short, grindingly hard, pervaded with mystery, and, for the most part, dull. Scientific advances have changed all that. Life today tends to be comfortable, reasonably long, not nearly so mysterious, and generally fascinating. With growing control over the environment comes a new sense of responsibility for human history, and this focus on present history is the genius of secularization. *Seculum* means "the present age," and this attention to the present stands in sharp contrast to the primary religious orientations that preceded it—first future into eternity and then backward into history. But it was during those past eras, the eschatalogical and the historical, that traditional Christian theology took shape. Today, the Church finds itself caught up in the radical reconstruction of theology, and the efforts being made at this reconstruction are called, somewhat inaccurately, the "New Theology."

How did traditional Christian theology take shape? It inherited its eschatological or forward-looking elements from the Jews. The messianic hope, which had its earliest and some of its finest expressions in the prophets (Isaish 2, 9, 11, 42, 50, 52-53; Jeremiah 23, 30, Micah 5, Ezekiel 34), was cherished through the years of foreign conquest that began in the eighth century B.C., to be reborn among the Jews in the third century

B.C. Between 200 B.C. and A.D.,100 there grew up a whole body of Jewish writings called *Apocalyptic*. Parts of the book of Daniel (e.g., chapter 7) are the earliest examples of this writing we have, and like all the rest of Jewish apocalyptic literature, they deal with the end of the world and what will come after it. They also lay great stress on the idea of divine intervention borrowed from the messianic hope.

At the same time Christian theology was assimilating these Jewish apocalyptic ideas (which are eschatological in their concern for "last things"), it was subject to other influences. From its Greco-Roman environment it took certain ideas and the vocabulary with which to express them. The idea of the "mutual in-dwelling" of the Father, Son, and Holy Ghost comes from the Greek word *perichoresis*. The relationship between the Father and Son within the Godhead is described by another Greek word, *homoousion*. The Greek term by which the second person of the Trinity is known, *logos* (meaning word), is a key word in traditional Christology. Still another source of influences that shaped the early development of traditional Christian theology were pagan philosophies. The word *logos* was a crucial term in Stoic philosophy, and other ideas borrowed from the pagan world are not hard to find. From the Manichaeans came the concept of dualism, the supernatural conflict of equally powerful forces of good and evil. From Platonism and Aristotelianism came certain ideas about natural and supernatural reality. What the Christian Church did was to borrow, modify, and adapt these disparate elements in order to explain and defend its faith against false teachings. This combining was done by the General Councils, the Scholastic movement and, to a lesser degree, the Renaissance humanists.

What were the steps in the development of traditional Christian theology? Generally speaking, before A.D. 313 the lordship of Jesus and his redemption of the world were accepted on faith. It was not until the fourth century, when pagan converts began to pour into the Church, that the problem of heresy became acute. The Church met this problem

The Development of Christian Theology 45

with a series of General Councils, and it may be valuable to review their major decisions. The first was held at Nicea in A.D. 325, convened by the Emperor Constantine. It attempted to deal with the Arian controversy. Arianism included the belief that Christ was created by God, and was therefore subordinate to the Father. Although Arianism had to be dealt with again by the next General Council, the Council of Nicea. did begin to define orthodoxy. Beginning with a brief baptismal creed (probably from Jerusalem), it added a statement describing the relationship of the Son to the Father as "being of one substance."

By 381, the climate of controversy had expanded to include along with Arianism two others: Macedonianism, which denied that the Holy Ghost is divine and Apollinarianism, which taught that the soul in man was replaced by God in Christ which would mean that Christ had no human soul—is not fully human. This belief is still common today, and it is utterly wrong. If Christ had no human soul, he would not have been fully human. Against all three heresies, the Council acted by expanding the creedal formula drawn up by the Council of Nicea to include assertions of the full humanity of Christ and the divinity of the Holy Ghost. This creed developed by the Council of Constantinople appears in the *Book of Common Prayer* (with a ninth century addition stating that the Holy Ghost "proceedeth from the Father *and the Son*") as the Nicene Creed.

However successful the Council of Constantinople was in refuting the heresies it faced, it did not preclude the possibility of new heresies. They soon appeared, and in various forms they are present even today. The first of these was Nestorianism. The Nestorians appeared to believe that there were two persons in Christ, one human and one divine. Jesus of Nazareth was not divine; he was simply "possessed" by a divine person within the Godhead much as you or I might be possessed by the Holy Ghost. The Council of Ephesus was convened to deal with Nestorianism and did so by reaffirming the Nicene Creed and declaring Nestorius' teaching false and accursed.

The next great heresy to be dealt with by a General Council was Monophysitism, the teaching that Christ had one, divine, nature. The Council of Chalcedon met in 451 to deal with this teaching and decreed that there were two natures in Christ, one human and one divine. In support of the full humanity of Christ, the Council proclaimed that "whatever of human nature Christ did not assume, he did not redeem."

The councils grew out of an earlier recognition by Christians that the end of the world would not come during their lifetimes. Therefore, it was necessary to put the essentials of the faith in writing for future generations. There theological significance lay in the facts that (1) they defined orthodox Christian faith in conformity with apostolic tradition, (2) they Hellenized the traditional expression of that faith, giving it a Greek framework of thought, and (3) they generated a new concern for supernaturalism as being continuous with the apostolic witness.

Just as there were other events occurring at the same time as the Conciliar Movement (the development of the Church calendar, for example), several concurrent events occupied the Middle Ages. In the development of Christian theology, the most important of these was Scholasticism. Scholasticism was the monastic development of Western Christian theology. During the Middle Ages, All scholarship was in monastic communities and, consequently, the particular genius of the Schoolmen (as the Scholastic monks are known) is the key to understanding our traditional theology. The aim of the schoolmen was the philosophical understanding of the faith. Their work gave rise to the stormy controversy between faith and reason.

The story of Scholasticism and its formative influence upon the faith can be most easily grasped in terms of the work of six men. First of these was St. Augustine (354-430), the bishop of Hippo in North Africa. It was he who first raised the issue of faith, reason, and will. Although convinced that man could not be saved by reason alone, he insisted that man could not be saved apart from reason. He further asserted that a third essential for salvation was the conversion of the will. God did indeed endow human beings with free will, but the will that moved them toward salvation had to be informed by and conformed to the love of God. Thus his dictum was, "Love God, and what you will, that do" (he is often misquoted as having said, "Love God and do as you please").

If Augustine was one of the pillars undergirding Scholasticism, Boethius (480?-524?) was the other. Boethius was a philosopher whose contribution was to impress medieval theology with Aristotelian thought. In his most famous work, *The Consolation of Philosophy*, he described the soul's attaining knowledge of the vision of God through philosophical speculation. The works of Augustine and Boethius started the fire of conflict between faith and reason that raged throughout the Middle Ages. It so influenced traditional Christian theology that the church was able to capitalize on the new learning of the Renaissance and thereby open itself to the subsequent tension between science and religion that lives at the heart of the secularist theology of our own day.

The problem of finding legitimate places for faith and reason to coexist within the structure of the Christian faith found a working solution in the eleventh century in the thought of St. Anselm (1033-1109) who, while he was archbishop of Canterbury, was a social reformer through whose influence England's activity in the slave trade was suppressed, His greatness is grounded in Anselm as philosopher and theologian. To him belongs the distinction of first codifying the rules by which reason would enquire legitimately into matters of faith. He regarded the role of philosophy as the understanding of what we believe. Thus, he developed the ontological argument, or the logical reasoning that supposedly leads one to belief in the existence of God. In his most celebrated work, *Cur Deus Homo?* he reinterpreted the doctrine of Atonement as a satisfaction paid to God for his outraged majesty rather than a ransom paid to the Devil. With Anselm, then, reason became increasingly a concrete ingredient of faith.

In the twelfth century, Peter Abelard (1079-1142) carried "liberalizing" process a step further by subjecting the doctrines of the Trinity and the Atonement to critical reason. After Abelard, no cherished belief was too sacred to be subjected to intellectual scrutiny. We can almost see in the contribution of Peter Abelard the completion of the cycle initiated by St. Augustine and Boethius six centuries earlier. They were the first to dignify the practice of applying reason to the article of Christian belief previously accepted on faith, but faith was still "holy ground" and reason trod lightly until Abelard released it to run to and from and assault even the high ground of man's faith in God.

About the same time, the first real secularist appeared in the person of Hugh of St. Victor (1096-1141). Hugh was a secularist to the extent of his conviction that the study of nature and the universe could supply valuable data about God. A scientist himself, he believed that the more a man could know about nature (which belonged to God), the more he could know of the mind of God. This was a penetrating insight, and its effect was to prepare the Church to accept and employ the new learning, which came with the Renaissance in the fourteenth century.

The last of the great Scholastics was also preeminently the theologian of the Renaissance, although he died just at the beginning of that era. He was St. Thomas Aquinas (1225-1274). The Renaissance period in European history, occurring roughly between the fourteenth and the seventeenth centuries, is of course best known as a time of renewed scholarly interest in antiquities. Greek philosophy has a new birth during the Renaissance, and the work of Aristotle became especially popular. This is significant in the development of traditional Western theology mainly because of its influence upon St. Thomas Aquinas. Among his distinctions is the fact that he brought the Scholastic movement to a close and codified and systemized Western theology so thoroughly that it underwent no further substantial development until the twentieth

The Development of Christian Theology 49

century. His great work of theological systematizing was the vast threepart *Summa Theologia*. The first two sections of this multi-volumed work have to do with the nature and being of God, and the third is a study of Christ as the means of human access to the Father. Thomas' work brings together the fundamental concerns of the Scholastic movement: faith; a Platonic world-view inherited from St. Augustine according to which our typical views of heaven and earth are shaped; and the rationalism of Aristotle. There is considerable irony in the fact that St. Thomas, who was above all the champion of the legitimate use of reason in questions of faith, was the man who brought the development of Christian theology in the West to a virtual standstill for seven hundred years. His work was so extensive and definitive that it was, in effect, *the official ruling* on nearly all theological issues down to the twentieth century. Roman Catholic theology is still largely "Thomistic," despite the work of the Second Vatican Council of 1964. It is quite apparent, however, that the Roman Catholic Communion views the present reconstruction of theology just as seriously as the rest of us and is also in a process of theological change. Western Christianity was so firmly grounded in Thomistic theology by the sixteenth century that the structure was able to withstand the pounding storm of the Reformation.

What was the philosophical shape of Thomistic theology? Briefly stated, it was, like the best of Scholastic theology, fundamentally concerned with ontology. Ontology is the study of *being* as such. It is the human effort to find meaning for existence within the comprehensive meaning of existence itself. Since God is the ultimate and independently existing Being and all other being or existence depends upon him, ontology is primarily concerned with the *being of God*, for he is the key to the meaning of all other forms of being. With this preoccupation about the nature and meaning of existence, traditional Christian theology emerged out of medieval Scholasticism with a hierarchical, or ladderlike, concept of being. God was at the top of the ladder as Independent Being. Beneath him on the ladder came the nine orders of angels. Beneath the angels came humanity, and beneath humanity, nature (animals, plants, and rocks). Then came a range of things that had a lesser hold on their own being—ideas and memories. Human beings related to God, nature, and the universe in terms of this "ladder of being." Each item has a firmer hold on its being than all that was below it. Thus, the higher a thing was on the ladder of being, the closer it was to God—from whom each creature receives its being—and the more real it was. The philosophical shape of traditional theology was therefore ontological. It was concerned with the nature of things, and the nature of things depended upon their relationship with God.

Out of this ontological concern for being, or for true nature of things, comes traditional Christian ethics with all its moral absolutes. We have already seen that the nature of things depended upon their relationship to God. On the level of intelligent beings, every relationship is a role we assume. We are faithful to the relationship as we fulfill its appropriate role (we are faithful to the marriage relationship, for example, as we fulfill our roles of husband and wife). Theologically and ontologically speaking, a human being is faithful in relationship to God when he or she fulfills his or her role as a human,

GOD INDEPENDENT BEING (ULTIMATE REALITY)
ANGELS (9 ORDERS)
HUMANITY
ANIMALS
PLANTS
MEMORIES, IDEAS* etc.

*Not to be confused with the Platonic doctrine of ideas.

a role that involves the proper use of life and all that belongs to life. Traditional Christian theology maintains that God made creation for humanity and humanity for God. The Westminster Confession describes human destiny in just this way: "The end of man is to enjoy God forever." St. Augustine said the same thing more poetically: "Thou hast made us for Thyself, O God; and our hearts are not at rest until they find rest in Thee." This is the presupposition that gives rise to the Christian ethic. If we insist that we have a destiny, it follows that whatever we do to advance toward that destiny is good and whatever we do to impede our progress toward that destiny is evil—or sin, which is moral evil. On this basis, we can make some general rules: there are some things which no one anywhere should ever do. These are valid generalizations, but to give them force Judaism and Christianity have both taught them as the Law of God. When you call such rules "the Law of God," they are not general rules. They are, in effect, absolute laws from which deviation becomes unthinkable.

"Thou shalt not take the Name of the Lord thy God in vain."
"Keep holy the Sabbath day."
"Honor thy father and thy mother."
"Thou shalt not commit adultery."
"Thou shalt not covet."

Over the centuries, these absolute moral prescriptions and proscriptions have had a beneficial effect upon society. Many of our laws and our social values are grounded in these religious commandments. The sanctity of marriage, of private property, of parental (and therefore of all property) authority were reinforced by God's Law, and that Law made possible the orderly, more-or-less stable development of society. Unfortunately, absolute moral laws are not always entirely beneficial. Modern psychoanalysis has shown that such absolute, perfectionist ethics can generate anxieties and hostilities, which twist and sicken people until they are no good to themselves or anyone else. This kind of psychological problem is generally not grounded in the nature of law or itself, but in the individual's own learning experience. Law is authority itself, but in the individual's own learning experience Law is good, but it has to be taught properly and applied properly or it becomes demonic. After all, as Jesus taught by working on the Sabbath, law was made for humanity, not humanity for law.

We have already seen how the traditional Christian ethic is grounded in an ontological concern, a concern for the true nature of things. Every person and everything has a characteristic nature and a characteristic function, purpose, behavior, or destiny. Since the being, or existence, of a person or thing includes its purpose or function, the characteristic function, or behavior can be described as the "natural law of its being." On the human level, we can say that natural law is behavior intended by the Creator as appropriate to a human being's true nature as a child of God. Below the human level, the natural law of a thing is its true use or purpose as intended by the Creator, which is communication. An ethical system that grows out of ontology will inevitably be an absolute, perfectionist ethical system because its "do's and don'ts" describe in black and white what is and what is not right for any class of existing things. Being ontological, traditional Christian ethics describes in black and white what is right conduct and what is wrong for the whole class of existing things called the human race.

All of us know that such an ideal ethic must cope with contradiction, but on the surface it cannot—it is not flexible enough. We may well believe that situations alter cases. We may be in full agreement with Sophocles, who said that "even though lying is generally wrong, when the truth involves hurt or ruin, then to lie is good." But ontological ethics say the perversion of language's function is the misuse of a Godgiven gift. To deal with this problem of conflicting "goods" Christianity developed a highly refined system of ethical decision-making apparatus called casuistry. Probably it is used most widely by priest-confessors to determine the rightness or wrongness of a penitent's action.

Traditional Christian ethics has given us some ground rules for use in those rare situations that require us to decide among alternatives, none of which are clearly good. The principle is to do that which admits of the greatest possible good. Observe how it can work.

Just before the close of World War II in Europe, an eighteen-year-old soldier was shot and mortally wounded. As he lay dying, as often happens, he cried for his mother. An elderly sergeant, hearing the boy's moaning plea, slithered over to him under the ceiling of shalls and shrapnel and, holding the boy in his arms said to him, "It's all right Son, Mother's here." And the young soldier died, feeling safe in his mother's arms. A literalistic, legalistic judgment on this might carry with it condemnation of the old sergeant on three counts: (1) he perverted the true purpose of speech, (2) he betrayed a dying comrade, and (3) he testified falsely about the presence of the boy's mother. But traditional Christian ethics is not blind and, according to its principle of choosing the greatest good, it would approve of the sergeant's conduct as being consistent with all that is best in humanity and God, namely love. Traditional Christian ethics would absolve the sergeant's lies as being evil but not sin. This distinction between *evil* (which is sometimes necessary) and *sin* (which is never necessary) is at the heart of our traditional Christian ethics. That ethics calls on people to be responsible in their choices, and in choosing, to do the best they can in the midst of evil—even bringing good out of evil, as the sergeant did.

Properly understood, traditional Christian ethics calls upon us to be faithful to our nature—to be human. It calls us to the dignity and accountability of responsible decision-making; to make choices in the clearest possible way; it confronts us with absolute laws that would dictate action according to the true nature of the being involved.

The application of traditional Christian ethics to the complex ethical questions we all face today is sometimes incredibly difficult—not because the choice is morally hard (though it may well be) but because the "right" choice is often so elusive.

54 THE CHURCH IN PERSPECTIVE

To say it more simply, traditional Christian ethics is cumbersome and highly complicated. This is the reason why traditional Christian ethics has been criticized and abandoned by many in recent years. The fact is that people today face moral issues that cannot be solved along the ontological lines that would tie us to the Middle Ages. Science has brought much of nature and history under human control. Because of this, the tension between science and religion is still with us, but for new reasons.

An example of an ethical problem insoluble along strictly ontological lines is the problem of overpopulation. These has never been any doubt that reproduction is among the basic human functions. In former times, a high birth rate was essential just to offset a high infant mortality rate, early adult death, and the scourge of fatal plagues. The Church felt compelled, for the good of society, to encourage large families. Medical and scientific advancement have gradually produced a radical change, however, and today the rate of human reproduction has so far outpaced the normal attrition of death that the entire world faces the serious prospect of famine. The eventual inability of the world to feed its population is a significant fact governing the Christian view of birth morality. Whereas it could once be said that a married couple capable of having children did wrong not to have as many as they could shelter, feed, clothe, and educate, such is no longer the case. It may in fact be the ultimate moral irresponsibility to have too many children.

Underlying this shift in the Christian ethical perspective is the intimate connection between the individual's duty (or rights) and the welfare of society. God, who cares for individuals, cares equally for their society. The fundamental problem of traditional Christian ethics, with its roots in ontological perspective that rigidly ties together function and existence is that there is litte flexibility to adapt to new conditions. Since Christianity cannot accept the concept of moral relativism (the view that there are no ethical absolutes), it has to establish a new ethical perspective of right and wrong. The complexity and sophistication of contemporary life confronts Christians not with the need to call yesterday's evil today's good, or vice versa, but honestly and openly to establish an ethical system that accounts for the new factors involved in responsible decision-making while remaining faithful to the highest principles of human behavior, love, and justice. Such an ethic will be grounded not just in the old ontological concern that restricts things to their obvious God-given use and purposes but rather in a secular, human-oriented concern that takes into consideration the situation and the possibilities contained in it. Thus, free to respond conscientiously to situations in terms of their own responsibilities and limitations, the Christians can take upon themselves the dignity of responsible and accountable decision-making, rather than be limited by a slavish obedience to codes which would confine decisions to the comparatively shallow depths of obedience or disobedience.

To say this is to describe a shift in ethical orientation from past expectations or future destiny to present possibilities—possibilities illuminated and informed by the love of God. This is consistent with a fundamental theological orientation which is secular, or grounded in this present age. It differs from the traditional orientation of Christian theology in that it is primarily concerned not with the meaning of existence, but rather with the meaning of experience. It is a radical break with the past because it constitutes a basic change in our religious viewpoint, or the way in which we understand ourselves and our behavior.

This secularization differs markedly from the humanism of the Renaissance because it necessitates the restructure of theology. Humanism, with its stress upon the ideals and interests of humanity rather than upon nature or God, is of enormous significance to the history of Christianity, but like the knowledge gleaned from modern depth psychologies, its insights could be quite adequately dealt with theoretically without altering the basic structure of that theology. To say this is to say a great deal about the comprehensiveness and sophistication of Christian theology at the time of the Renaissance, for the fundamental contradiction between theology and humanism was not in the realm of subject matter or content, it was in the philosophical realm. Christian theology was largely Aristotelian; humanism was Platonic. The significance of the difference is illustrated by the Aristotelian versus the Platonic doctrine of ideas.

The Platonic system regarded every existing thing as an imperfect representation of the perfection of its kind of thing (which existed in the realm of ideas and contained the essential nature of that particular class of thing). The desk in which I am writing is a desk (ideal) that possesses in highest degree every essential of "deskly" perfection. My existing desk lacks the excellence of the perfect desk, but it is a good desk to the degree in which it conforms to the idea of what it means for a thing to be perfectly a desk. The Aristotelian system did not admit of this separation between essence (what constitutes a true desk) and existence (the fact that a thing called a desk actually rather than potentially exists).

Humanism did not change the Church's traditional theology, but it did challenge the Church's authority, doing so on the basis of the new learning of the Renaissance. Humanism began a liberalizing trend, and that trend ultimately led to the Reformation. As proof that humanism did not alter greatly traditional Christian theology, witness the fact that the Reformation it made possible was primarily "political," not theological. In rebelling against the claims of the papacy, the Reformers raised only four theological issues: (1) papal supremacy and monarchy, (2) free will and predestination, (3) good works and salvation, and (4) the papal doctrine of transubstantiation.

We have already observed that the secular concerns, orientation, and assumptions of today confront the Church with the serious task of theological reconstruction if it is to speak meaningfully to contemporary man. Out of this concern to reconstruct Christian theology along secular lines came the "New Theology." There are many who would describe it as simply a crude effort on the part of a few theologians to assimilate and "Christianize" the existentialist preconceptions of Martin Heidegger, Jean-Paul Sartre, and others. Existentialism is secular. It stresses the importance of personal encounter, basic honesty, and unimpaired free will. It is dramatically opposed to ethical codes and slavish conformity, and it rejects passionately the supernaturalism of traditional Christianity. But the New Theology is not existentialism. Existentialism is a modern European philosophical and literary movement that flourished, especially in France, after World War II. It was an outgrowth of the pain and disillusionment of war and expressed a loss of faith in humanity as much as a denial of God. It viewed the human existential (or presently existing) situation with profound despair. Religious agnosticism, if not outright atheism, was a part of that despair because the traditional religious claims for God flew in the face of the tragic and contradicting data of life.

The philosophy of existentialism is important to the history of religious thought because it came as the first sign that a new era of secular Christian theology was at hand. The new era was predicted most eloquently by Dietrich Bonhoeffer, a young Lutheran pastor martyred by the Nazis on April 9, 1945, just before the close of the war. Shortly before his execution, he wrote to a friend his view of the coming religious ferment: "We are coming to a time of no religion at all. How can we speak of God without religion?" In another letter, he saw that the coming ferment would encompass more than a crisis of religious language, that the world of tomorrow would be a world in which human beings would determine the course of history and control much of nature. In such a world, people would not easily feel any need for or dependence upon God. Bonhoeffer's realism breathes of anguish in the question he raised: "How is faith possible in a world that does not need God?"

This school of theology took shape among professional theologians away from public view. Public awareness of what it was and what it meant awaited the publication in 1963 of

Anglican Bishop John A. Robinson's book, *Honest to God*. The book is not a scholarly work, but a sharing of Bishop Robinson's own reflections, and it may well prove to have been one of the dozen most important religious works of this century. It opened to public awareness the storm of theological reform that has battered the Church's institutions. The storm has had good effects. It has ended a "drought" that reduced the Church's theological creativity to one field—though a very important one—biblical scholarship.

The key phrase in all of Christian theology is "the Word became flesh" (St. John, chapter 1). On the truth of that phrase depends everything that Christianity teaches. The phrase confronts us with the two concerns always most important to Christian theology equally basic to the new theological schools. These concerns are the doctrine of God and the relationship of Creator to creation. Since our traditional doctrine of God is Trinitarian, let us now consider it in some detail.

"All that God does, the whole Trinity does." That sentence sounds radical and seems to carry with it the threat of merging the three Persons of the Trinity into one. It sounded radical when it was first uttered in the beginning of the fifth and twentieth, people have been more likely to separate the Persons of the Trinity than to merge them, and in practice most people think of three gods, not one.

What does the doctrine of the Trinity really mean? It doesn't mean anything unless we understand what it is. It is a statement that describes God in terms of humanity's total experience of God. The doctrine of the Trinity cannot be understood apart from human experience. Let me illustrate. No matter what else you think about God, there is a sense in which he is completely different from what you are. You are a creature of time. You have a past, a present, and a future. That is the first difference: God has no past and no future. God is not a creature of time—so all events, all of history, are a present experience to God. Thus it was appropriate for Jesus Christ to assert his unity with the Father in the shocking words, "Before Abraham was, I am" (St. John 8:58). Another difference is that we all have some limit to what we know. Not only do we not know everything, we cannot now remember a lot of what we once did know. God knows all. He is, we say, omniscient, and that is quite a difference between God and each of us. Other differences are equally great. We, for example, can be in only one place at one time. God is everywhere. He is omnipresent. We could go on heaping up examples to show how God and we are different, but it is enough to say that you and I have our limits, but God is *limitless*. The first thing the doctrine of the Trinity says about God is that he is enormously different from what we are.

To say how God is different from us is not to say all there is of our experience of God. We know that he is also intensely like us. Look at yourself again. You are aware of feeliings of love and of anger. Love and anger are a part of God's life, too. You have a certain amount of freedom—freedom to choose how you will live, what you will or will not do, and what you will be. Likewise, freedom and choice belong to God. Then there is the one great thing we all have in common, our very humanity. We not only have our humanity in common with each other, we have humanity in common with God. Think about that. This is the meaning of Christmas. When we call Christ "very God of very God," we do not mean that through Christ God was "dipped" in humanity the way we might dip a nut in chocolate. We mean that in Jesus Christ God took our humanity into himself. We prefer to think of Christ's divinity, but maybe his humanity is more important, because it is in Christ's humanity that God is intensely like us. Have you ever been lonely, embarrassed, or afraid? God knows what lonliness is, and he knows what it means to be afraid and embarrassed. Ever been on a diet? God knows what human hunger feels like. Here then are ways in which God is so much like us it hurts!

We still have not said all we can about God. It isn't enough just to point out the ways in which God is different from us and the ways in which he is like us. There is more to people's experience of God than a lot of similarities and differences.

There is another whole area of experience people have had with God, and it is one they have learned to take very seriously. It is the experience of God's present influence. Influence is a powerfully real force. You can see how it works by noticing teenagers who have come under the influence of one of their music heroes. They cut their hair the same way, they dress the same way, and they even speak the same way. They are the same kids they were before, but they seem to express something of the presence of their heroes. Admittedly, this is a rather crude example of the differences that influence can make on a person, but all influence works the same way. It changes the way we express ourselves. It even changes the things we do. Outwardly, it seems to change us through and through, although we really remain the same persons. Any teaching about God that fails to take account of his present influence upon people would be incomplete, because that influence is a part of people's real-life experience. The doctrine of the Trinity deals with this ever-present influence of God by speaking of the action of the Spirit of God, the Holy Spirit, and the influence of the Holy Spirit is what we call *grace*.

Traditionally, Christianity has viewed the doctrine of the Trinity as the only adequate and true description of God—all other views have been condemned. The new theologians do not deny, universally or necessarily the doctrine of the Trinity, but regard it as a sort of working hypothesis. In common with traditional theology, this recent trend sees the "connective" between Creator and creation to be Christ. This means that the "New Theology" might best be called "Christology." The "New Theology" sees the traditional Christian doctrine of God to be meaningless, quite apart from its trinitarian formula, because of its dual emphasis upon God's transcendence (his being supernatural and therefore different from human beings) and his being active within the field of human history. The "New Theology" tends to rethink supernatural ideas about God, insisting that all we know about him is what we know about Christ. Against the traditional view that history is the stage upon which the drama of God's activity is played, the "New Theology" tends toward the theory that the course of history is not in God's hand alone, but perhaps more directly in the hands of human beings. And, as well as being responsible for the course of history, growing scientific sophistication is making humanity increasingly responsible for nature as well. The conviction that what was once God's part in history and nature is being taken over increasingly by human beings has as its corollary the fact that God's transcendence and his supernatural power become less apparent in history and nature, they become less and less meaningful for us. Humanity's ascendence would seem to have made it impossible to say much more about God that we can actually say about Christ.

In other words, the "New Theology," agrees with traditional Christian theology in its insistence that Christ is central to any adequate concept of God. What seems to preoccupy the new theologians about God is his transcendence, or to put it more simply, his supernatural existence. Since they tend to reject supernaturalism as the grounds upon which people can know God, what is at issue is not the divinity of Christ but the humanity of God as we know it through Christ.

Against this trend, we have seen recently a resurgence of fundamentalism within the traditional catholic churches. This has manifested itself in several ways—biblical, and theological literalism and a sometimes reactionary appeal to tradition.

One final word—life in Christ, whether radical or conservative, cannot normally exist apart from the Body of Christ—the Church.

Further study in recent theological developments can be done under the direction of your bishop.

III. LITURGICAL WORSHIP

In the minds of many Christians, The Church is the repository of timeless and eternal truths. It is thought to be relatively as stable and changeless in its institutional make-up as is the faith on which it stands. Paradoxically, the history of the Church is the story of almost constant change—even in its manner of worship.

We call the corporate worship of the Church liturgical worship. Liturgy in its original Greek form means "peoples work" or "public work." So when we speak of liturgical worship, we are talking about the ordered way Christians worship together in groups. Most social customs have changed over the years, and it should come as no surprise that liturgical customs change with the passing generations, too. To Christians whose parishes have been engaged in liturgical renewal, the idea of change is not new and, since the Second Vatican Council, we all have heard something about liturgical change in our sister communion, the Roman Catholic Church. Probably, few of us are aware of the radical change that has been going on within the American branch of the Anglican Communion throughout its relatively short lifetime. In about

130 years, a host of things have intruded themselves into Episcopal worship services which we now take for granted as being characteristic of the Episcopal Church, never realizing that to Episcopalians a century ago they were new, strange, and not always appreciated.

We can dramatize this liturgical change by painting a word picture of an Episcopal Church today, italicizing the changes made in the last 130 years: *Altar, altar crosses, altar candles, flowers, vested clergy, vested choir, acolytes, Book of Common Prayer, pulpit.* There has not only been considerable change in our branch of the Anglican Church in a dozen or so decades, but it has been very basic change in almost every instance. In the 1860's, a midwestern bishop addressed a pastoral letter to his diocese in which he said "If there is an altar cross in my diocese, I will have that cross removed if it costs me my [episcopate]." The General Convention of 1871 was petitioned to forbid the use of acolytes to assist the clergy in services of public worship. And a hundred years ago, for the clergy to celebrate Holy Communion with their *backs* toward the congregation was a real innovation. Therefore, even in the Episcopal Church in America, liturgical renewal is not new.

The story of the liturgical history of the Church can be told on four parts: worship in the early Church, worship during the Middle Ages, worship in the Reformation and, finally, Anglican Prayer Book worship.

Worship in the Early Church and During the Middle Ages

The early Christian Church went through a cultural change from Jewish to Gentile membership that profoundly affected its worship life. The first Christians were Jews—all of them—and they observed the same worship life which all good Jews of the first century did. What distinguished them as Christians was that they added to their Jewish faith belief in Jesus as the promised Messiah of God, and they celebrated the eucharist, or Holy Communion. From its Jewish origins, Christianity inherited two things: a theology of sacrifice borrowed from temple worship—in the light of which Christ's death was understood—and an eschatological concern (the concern for the last things, the end of the world). The early Christians believed the end of the world and the Second Coming of Christ to be just around the corner. To be obsessed with getting to God in eternity was, therefore, not morbid but prudent.

There really is no Christian theology of sacrifice: our sacrificial theology is Jewish, and the genius of it is representational not substitutionary. A sacrificial animal was not offered as a substitute for the worshiper's life; it represented the worshiper's life. We understand sacrament to be a symbol by means of which we accomplish something of deep inner meaning. As we venerate and adore our Lord in the sacraments or symbols, we actually accomplish what we set out to do, to honor Christ and enjoy his presence. This Judaeo-Christian sacrificial theology (generally called sacramental theology in Christian circles) involves three essential steps: (1) the worshiper identifies with the victim—its life represents his own, (2) he offers to God, under the symbol of the animal's life, his own life—his most precious gift—by slaying the beast, and (3) finally, by feasting on the flesh of the sacrificed animal, communion between God and the worshiper is effected. What belongs to God (the sacrificed life) is received back by the worshiper holy and sinless for having belonged to God.

This sacrificial Jewish theology was the logical framework for the Christian understanding of the death of our Lord, especially since the first generation of Christians were themselves Jews. This sacrificial theology is important for understanding the eucharist, but it not the background out of which the eucharistic rite emerged. The model on which the Last Supper of our Lord, and every eucharist since, was based was a Jewish religious meal called a *chaburah* (pronounced ka-boo-rahk). Chaburoth, the plural form of the word, were small groups of ten or a dozen men that formed within the larger fellowship of the congregation for purposes of devotion or charity. They were groups of male friends (which is what the root meaning of the word is) who shared, by means of table fellowship and worship, a sense of identity and mutual support. The chaburah is the context in which the eucharist was concieved, for the Last Supper was a caburah meal.

This is not enough to describe the origins of our eucharistic worship adequately, however, because the eucharist is really not one service but two. The sacrificial Jewish theology of temple worship forms a part of the rationale for the second part of the service, the part modeled on the chaburah, which is the communion itself. But the first part of Holy Communion has little to do with sacrifice. It is a service of prayer, Scripture reading, and preaching. This much of the Communion service (which, in its present form, goes through the Creed) is called Ante-Communion. It can stand alone as a separate service and, like the Communion itself, it has its roots buried in Judaism—in this case in synagogue worship) and the Communion itself (based on the chaburah).

The transition of Christianity from a Jewish sect to a Gentile religion was, as we have seen, fraught with all kinds of problems. For example, because the first form of corporate worship was the Holy Communion (which continued to be the normal form of Sunday worship for Christians until the Reformation), and because during the first century the communion really involved a meal, there were serious problems. They arose with the missionary work of St. Paul, for Paul made converts of Gentiles without first requiring that they become Jews, and Jewish Christians felt themselves forbidden to have communion with the new Gentile converts because the law forbade Jews to eat with Gentiles. This problem of table fellowship was so great a crisis for the young church that a council of the Apostles was convened at Jerusalem in A.D. 49 to settle the matter of whether or not converts to Christianity should be required to become Jews first. The fifteenth chapter of the Acts of the Apostles tells the story of the crises, the council, and the compromise worked out. It was over this issue that St. Peter and St. Paul fell out. The Council, which was presided over by St. James, decided that Gentile converts need *not* first become Jews in order to join the Christian Church. St. James was a relative of our Lord (perhaps a brother or cousin) and apparently the head of the Church at that time.[1] The significance of the decision of the Council of Jerusalem was that it saved Christianity from being nothing other than a minor Jewish sect.

We have already observed that Sunday worship in the early Church consisted of a service of the eucharist. During the first two centuries A.D., there were very few documents written to tell us what the communion service was like. St. Paul describes the service in outline in the eleventh chapter of the First Epistle to the Corinthians. In the second century Justin Martyr, a layman, theologian, and, finally, a martyr, wrote a quite thorough description of the service as it was observed in Rome. The eucharist Justin describes does agree in the essentials with the eucharistic action which is a part of the communion celebration today. There were slight but important differences, however, and these Richard Spielmann treats with clarity and precision in his *History of Christian Worship*.[2] Most of them had to do with the order of things. From the third century, a document called "The Apostolic Tradition," written by Hippolytus, a Roman priest, gives us a much fuller insight into the early eucharist. His description agrees in essentials with Justin Martyr's but gives more detail—even quoting the prayers used. These and other records indicate that normal Sunday worship in the early Church was Holy Communion, and

---

1. Saint Peter, often characterized as "The Prince of the Apostles," was not at that time the leader of the Church and, although a leading figure in the faction opposed by Saint Paul, earlier demonstrated a vacillation that was hardly worthy of a leader in any cause (Acts 10:48; Galatians 1 and 2).

2. (New York, 1966).

the service as we have it today contains every essential of that used by the first Christians. The Communion today differs somewhat from its form in the first three centuries, but the changes have been additions—nothing has been lost. The changes appeared during the Middle Ages and were of two kinds: ceremonial actions and penitential mood.

It is understandable that the Middle Ages should have given us liturgical changes, for the Church was changed in many other ways that affected profoundly what it believed and practiced. The legalizing of Christianity in the fourth century by the Emperor Constantine precipitated a period of dramatic growth. This was itself the cause of a liturgical change, namely the separation of the parts of the individual's initiation rite. During the centuries of persecution, initiates were adults. The period of preparation was long—two or three years in most places. The service of initiation was a fitting climax to those years. Baptism, confirmation, and first communion—the initiation had three parts—but they were parts of one, single worship event. They took place on Easter or Pentecost in the early morning. Generally speaking, baptism was administered in a suitable place away from the congregation, the ministers being deacons. The candidates, who were nude, were baptized by total immersion (aspersion, or "sprinkling," came into use during the Middle Ages for reasons of convenience). Immediately after baptism, the candidate, clothed in a white garment, symbolizing purity, would go into the main body of the congregation in whose presence he would be confirmed by the bishop. After the candidates had all been confirmed they would then receive their first Holy Communion, with milk and honey as well as bread and wine.

After the Christian Church was legalized in 313, however, it became impossible to cope with the great number of candidates on this basis. Gradually, between the fourth and ninth centuries, the separation of baptism and confirmation came about. The theory was that the bishop could delegate authority to priests in local congregations to perform the first part of the initiation, and the second part would then await an occasional visit by the bishop. This opened the way for infant baptism that became a lively option when the prolonged preparation required in a time of persecution was no longer essential.

Other changes came into being about this time also. Among them was the physical place in which liturgical worship of the congregation occurred. In the days of the early Church, Christian worship took place in houses—frequently in private homes belonging to members of the congregation. After the Christian Church was legalized and its dramatic growth had begun, there was need for larger facilities, and the Church set about putting up church buildings as such. The first church buildings, which date from the fourth century, were like sheds or warehouses and are called basilicas.

These public buildings brought with them certain possibilities for the expansion of worship. Prayers, which up to this time were somewhat spontaneous, began to assume set forms. The Church began to develop music for use in its worship life, and made the service, which was always sung, increasingly elaborate. This is an important point and the reader should make note of it. In the normal life of the Christian Church, the weekly eucharists were always sung until sometime around the thirteenth century. So what we see in the development of church music is the embellishment of that service, and the service became somewhat more lengthy. In the early Church, the eucharist was a good deal shorter than it is in its present form. During the time of the persecutions, Christians were obviously not anxious to have their connection with the Church noticed, and so they worshiped very plainly. After the Church became legalized, began to have its own buildings, and to elaborate on its services, it became customary for the officers of the eucharist, the clergy, to wear suitable garments—a liturgical uniform. There was biblical precedent for this, because King Solomon, in dedicating the Temple of Jerusalem (I Kings 8) had arrayed himself in splendid garments. The garments that the Church used were variations of the layman's garments in the Roman Empire. This was the beginning of church vestments.

Perhaps during the Middle Ages, the change in mood of the Communion service was a more important change than any of the trappings that attached to it—more important than buildings and vestments or any of these things. In the early church, the eucharist was a service of thanksgiving—this is what eucharist means in Greek. The whole tone of it was one of gratitude—the grateful offering to God of the things that God had given to man. This changed in the Middle Ages, gradually but profoundly, and it is not easy to say why. The temper of the times was such that people became enormously concerned with the meaning of things. The Christian faith itself had no real theology until the Middle Ages, but with ill-prepared pagans being baptized and taking their places within the Christian family, their half-Christianized ideas gave birth to heresies or false teachings to which the Church had to respond. In response to those heresies, the Church had to develop an orthodoxy of theology, a system of belief consistent with the faith delivered to the first Apostles. Developing that theology was like setting a hayfield on fire; it was easier to begin the process than it was to control it or bring it to an end. Indeed, the theological development of Christianity has not yet been brought to an end and never will be.

A eucharistic theology, or a concern for what to believe about the eucharist, gave rise to a theology that fastened on not just *what* happens but *when*. It was a small step from believing in the Real Presence of Christ to wanting to establish the precise moment at which the Real Presence became a fact. This concern is the background against which the doctrine of transubstantiation was developed. Transubstantiation is the belief that with the consecration of the elements in Communion they become part of the flesh and blood of Jesus Christ, although retaining the outward appearance of bread and wine. The concern with the presence of Christ enhanced enormously the stature of the clergy, because the priest was the man who was able to accomplish the "miracle of the altar." This set the clergy apart from the laity in people's minds and began a dichotomy that the churches have had to live with ever since. It began an ecclesiastical hierarchy who mediated between the laity and God. In such a role, they succeeded in instilling in the minds of the laity a sense of unworthiness and a penitential sense that was not a part of the eucharistic worship of earlier Christians. The joy and thanksgiving of earlier times went out of the eucharist and was replaced with a sense of penitence and unworthiness.

Another development of the Middle Ages actually had its roots in the third century. It was the service of the Divine Office. The Divine Office was actually a series of little sung services of prayer, Scripture, canticles, and psalms recited throughout the whole course of the day. The Divine Office was first mentioned in the *Apostolic Tradition* of Hippolytus, a third century book already mentioned, which lists the canonical hours of the Divine Office. There were eight of them: *Vigil*, held during the night, on the eve of a feast day; *Matins*, at cockcrow, or sunrise; *Prime*, in the morning on rising or shortly thereafter; *Terse*, at third hour, or at nine o'clock as we would know it; *Nones*, at ninth hour, or what we would call three o'clock; *Vespers*, in the evening; and *Compline*, at midnight. These services were regularly observed by people in religious orders. Today, they are observed by monks and nuns almost exclusively, although not all religious orders observe all eight canonical hours.

These services of the Divine Office were, like the eucharistic worship of congregations, sung, not spoken. The music that accompanied church worship was, throughout the Middle Ages, very plain. In fact, the polyphonic music that we think of as normal church music today really dates from the seventeenth century. Before that, plain song, or the chanting that accompanied the service, was much simpler.

The first services to be spoken were eucharists, about the thirteenth century. They were private services, generally masses for the dead. Spielmann's *History of Christian Worship* contains an outstanding account of why this transition occurred and what the theology of the spoken service was. As Spielmann explains, with the doctrine of transubstantiation there came about an enormous awareness of Christ's physical presence in the bread and wine to seeing the eucharist itself as the reoffering of Christ. The Church never taught officially that Christ was sacrificed anew at each eucharist, but there came to be a tacit belief on the part of ignorant and many in the laity that this in fact is what the eucharist meant. Unlearned clergy, and the laity in general, came to believe that as our Lord was repeatedly sacrificed at each eucharist, some merit would attach to the worshipers who participated in that redeeming act. This view implied that offering the eucharist was a kind of good work and that certain merit attached to the worshiper of Christianity (who didn't have to be present or even alive to receive that benefit) with each such offering. When this belief became widely current, buying private masses which the clergy would then simply *say* rather than *sing*—without a congregation and without a choir—became common practice. Of course, the reader will recognize the theological problem. The sacrifice of the eucharist is not the reoffering of our Lord who, as we say in the Communion service, offered on his cross "one full, perfect and sufficient sacrifice, oblation and satisfaction for the sins of the whole world." His one offering was entirely adequate for everyone, everywhere, in every age, and needs no repetition. To hold a doctrine that Christ's sacrifice needs to be—or even can be—repeated, is blasphemously to imply that the event once enacted on Calvary was inadequate.

The last liturgical development during the Middle Ages with which we will concern ourselves had to do with the increasing hierarchicalism, or clericalism, of the Church. Gradually over the centuries there came into being the belief that the laity should *observe* the eucharist but not participate in it. They were excluded not only from receiving the chalice, but also from meaningful participation in the service. The service continued to be celebrated in Latin, a tongue foreign to most of the laity by the ninth century, and that was a further barrier to their understanding or involvement. The frequency with which the laity received Communion declined to once a year, if that. The eucharist became the priest's business, with the people left to engage in their own private devotions.

Although it is true that corporate worship deteriorated in the quality and amount of congregational participation in the Middle Ages and that the Middle Ages also saw the descent into corruption of the papacy, the reader should bear in mind that the medieval Church was not without its saints, and that the development of theology within the scholarly circles of monasticism continued unabated.

Worship and the Reformation

The Reformation was primarily concerned not with worship, but with the abuses of papal authority we have already considered. By the time of the Reformation, the clergy were absolutely central to the Church's corporate worship. What the clergy did was thought more important than what the congregation did, and the frequency of individual communions declined during the Middle Ages.

The reformers were immensely concerned with teachings and practices attached to the eucharist. Martin Luther, for example, was concerned with the sale of eucharists and with the whole concept of the eucharist's being offered as a work obtaining merit for the worshiper. This was all bound up with the same protest he lodged against the sale of indulgences. Like all the other Reformers, Martin Luther could not accept the doctrine of transubstantiation. His own doctrine of eucharist was somewhat conservative, and not entirely unrelated to transubstantiation, but rejecting the belief that the bread and wine become literally the body and blood of Jesus, he set a precedent for all the other reformers.

They followed in more liberal paths. To Martin Luther, the eucharist was still the normal form of congregational worship.

Since congregational participation in the eucharist (and especially in receiving the Holy Communion) had in the Middle Ages become highly irregular on the part of the laity, people did not feel attached to it in the way that early Christians were. Many of the reformers, for example Zwingli, replaced the eucharist with a Sunday service of preaching, prayer, and Scripture reading. Of course, this changed the mood to one of edification and instruction rather than adoration and worship. John Calvin was not particularly interested in liturgy, probably because his interests as a lawyer were in doctrine and conduct. When he went to Geneva, where he preached and taught, he made the normal Sunday service a preaching service in the tradition of Zwingli. No doubt the presence of such a service reflected the influence in Geneva of one of Zwingli's disciples, William Farel. For the most part, Protestant churches were preaching churches, not eucharistic churches. They did tend to be liturgical churches, however, and they had or came to have books describing the forms of worship they used.

One of the most significant liturgical developments of the Reformation, though, was the creation of so-called free worship churches, or churches that worshiped without any set liturgical forms. They began to have routine patterns and emphasis, but not liturgy as we know it. These churches were not uncommon on the continent, or in Scotland and England, where they were even popular. They were, in some sense, congregational, at least to the extent that the local congregation was the authoritative body in deciding matters of worship. Moreover, they tended to be fundamentalistic: they took every word of the Bible as literally the word of God and they were concerned to be spontaneous in the expression of their worship. They were immensely concerned with the inspiration of the Holy Spirit in the experience if the individual worshiper and they believed that various kinds of spontaneous or extemporary prayer were evidence of the inspiration of the Holy Ghost. Therefore, they placed a great stress upon such prayer.

Liturgical Worship 75

To the liturgical developments of the Reformation there was a vigorous Roman Catholic response. After the Reformation, we must begin to distinguish Western Catholicism and Roman Catholicism because there were other bodies, particularly the Anglican, validly claiming to continue their Catholic heritage, but standing in sharp distinction to anything that spoke of obedience to papal authority. The Counter-Reformation in the sixteenth century saw the Roman Catholic Church attempt to entrench its most conservative forms of worship and conduct, and thereby to implement the defense of its own tradition against the innovations of Protestantism. In 1570, Pope Pius V prescribed the use of a uniform Roman Missal, which had the stabilizing effect on the Roman liturgy. In the centuries that followed, Roman Catholic practice, which continued its medieval traditions, gradually went through another stage of great elaboration.

In the seventeenth, eighteenth, and nineteenth centuries, the Roman Church developed several means by which it could occupy the attention of the laity during mass and even achieve their edification in some measure. The use of colorful vestments was elaborated further. Church interiors were embellished with paintings and statues to capture the imagination and inspire the devotion of the laity. Ceremonies were adorned with complicated and difficult choir music. Holy water, with which the layman would wash ceremonially and cleanse himself upon entering the church, came into almost universal use. The effect of such innovations was twofold: the increasing hierarchicalism of the Church and the exclusion of the laity from participation or position within it. During the Middle Ages, the laity had become accustomed to second-class membership in the Body of Christ. From the seventeenth to nineteenth centuries, the priesthood became a virtual princedom of clergy in whose possession were all the trappings of pomp, prestige, and spiritual power. Against this sad background, the earliest development of the Anglican tradition is to be seen. The story of Anglicanism is best told in terms of the *Book of Common Prayer*.

The story of the Prayer Book, like the story of the vernacular Bible and its possession by the laity, is a huge study worthy of the years of scholarly effort that have gone into it and the almost uncountable number of books and papers that have come out of that work. It is difficult to reduce such large problems to manageable proportions. But the purpose of this work is to provide minimum breadth rather than maximum depth and give the reader a working perspective of the Episcopal Church faithful to its history and adequate to the needs of and ministry in contemporary American society. Thus, we will proceed with our survey of the *Book of Common Prayer* in terms of the several editions of the Prayer Book adopted for official use, their differences, and the background of politics and religion that gave rise to them. Politics and religion belong together simply because the history of the Church of England, the "mother" church of the worldwide Anglican Communion, is the history of an established, state Church. No Church is without its politics, but the politics of an established Church are the politics of the realm in which it exists.

Anglican Prayer Book Worship

The story of Anglican Prayer Book worship is complicated. Actually, it is two stories; first the English *Book of Common Prayer* was written, then much later, the American. In England, the story of Prayer Book worship has to be understood in terms of the climate of Protestant-Catholic conflict that characterized the sixteenth and seventeenth centuries. Politics loomed large in this development since the Church of England was, at the time, the only one legally franchised in England and, as an established Church, was under the administration of the Crown and Parliament.

Liturgical reform in England, of which Thomas Cranmer was the chief architect, dates from the reign of Henry VIII, although under Henry's rule it was slight. He allowed English to be used in services and, in 1544, permitted Cranmer to write and publish the first English-language litany. Although Cranmer had been considerably influenced by Protestant theology, Henry VIII remained a strict Catholic. Henry was also a brilliant theologian and not one to have anything changed without his approval. Further liturgical reform, therefore, awaited the reign of his successor.

The new sovereign who succeeded in 1547 was Edward VI. Edward was a child, and during his reign England was governed by a regency, a body of governors, most of whom were Protestant. Among the general population, there was a broad spectrum of religious opinion. Basically, there were three religious parties; the conservatives who were distinctly Catholic though not necessarily papalist, the reformed Catholic group, and a reforming group of radicals who were mostly Calvinists. Cranmer was a moderate reformer; Henry VIII had been a conservative. Cranmer was a speculative politician, and he succeeded in using the regency to accomplish his reforms.

In 1547, Parliament enacted a law stating that the chalice should *not* be withheld from the laity at the Holy Communion. In order to give them the chalice, however, a new eucharistic form was needed, for the form then in use made no such provision. Here, then, was the clear need for liturgical revision, and it led, in 1549, to the first *Book of Common Prayer*. In writing the book, Cranmer made use of ancient sources, and, although he was quite amenable to contemporary Protestant influence, the 1549 book was plainly Catholic. As has every subsequent Prayer Book, it contained the daily office of Morning and Evening Prayer, although Morning Prayer was not intended to be the regular Sunday morning worship for parish congregations. Sunday morning worship continued to be the mass.

Since the Reformation in England was more political than theological, Cranmer never lost sight of political realities. Although himself a moderate reformer, he had hoped that the

78 THE CHURCH IN PERSPECTIVE

Prayer Book of 1549 would find acceptance among all parties. Unfortunately, the conservatives thought it too reformed and the reformed party reacted against it because of its catholicism. All scholars agree that the book actually was a catholic document.

The Prayer Book that followed it in 1552 was not. The political climate continued to change in the direction of reform after 1549 and Cranmer's second Prayer Book reflects this change as well as his own Protestant inclination. The scholarly consensus is that the Prayer Book of 1552 was clearly inferior to the the 1549 book. More than the first Prayer Book, the second was sort of a catholic-reformed hodgepodge intended to please everyone. Like the earlier book, it was not acceptable to any party and it was never approved by the Church. Most of its radical alterations had to do with the eucharist. It called for the celebrant to wear a surplice in place of a chasuble; it deleted the introit, Kyrie, and Gloria in Excelsis, prayers for the dead, and the requirement of kneeling to receive the sacrament. The words of administration were changed from "The Body (The Blood) of our Lord Jesus Christ which was given for thee..." to "Take and eat this in remembrance..." and "Drink this in remembrance...." To the services of Morning and Evening Prayer were added the penitential openings so much in keeping with reformed attitudes.

The Prayer Book of 1552 had no official Church approval and less than a year of use in England. In 1553, Edward VI died and was succeeded by Mary Tudor, daughter of Henry VIII. Her first act was to restore the Roman Catholic faith and obedience in England. Bishops, clergy, and others to whom papal obedience was intolerable fled to Holland and Geneva and there came into close contact with Calvinism. They made use of the 1552 Prayer Book during their period of exile, which ended in 1558. In that year another daughter of Henry VIII came to the throne—Elizabeth I. She restored the Church of England, and in so doing faced a leadership crisis, which helped to determine the shape of Anglicanism from that day to this. The papalist bishops and clergy appointed by Mary were unwilling to give up their allegiance to the pope and, therefore, had to be replaced. The only churchmen whom Elizabeth could appoint in their places were the reformers who in Mary's reign had been in exile on the continent. These brought to the church a strong evangelistic tradition, from which the *Low Church* faction of later days emerged. The traditional, catholic members coalesced in the *High Church* faction. Elizabeth I was herself a catholic, but she knew she would have to avoid either extreme if she would unite her people, whose doctrinal sensitivities ranged from protestant to papal. She quickly discerned that since doctrinal agreement among her subjects was not possible, common worship was the principle upon which religious unity (and political stability) would have to be built. Part of the genius with which this was achieved was the creation of a "bridge church," a church with a clearly reformed polity at the center of which its catholic heritage and Apostolic Succession found vigorous expression.

The reestablishment of the English Church under Elizabeth I brought into being another edition of the Prayer Book, the edition of 1559. A compromise between the extreme catholicism of the 1549 book and the protestantism of the 1552 book, it was actually closer to the 1552 edition. The book was used until the Commonwealth Period, 1649-1660, during which the monarchy was suppressed, King Charles I was beheaded, and the Church of England was replaced with a congregational presbyterianism. Why this repudiation of crown and established church came about cannot detain us here, but the Anglican lay reader should become familiar with the basic issue, the divine right of kings. Charles I was the last of England's great absolute rulers. He believed himself above the law, and thus flew in the face of the inexorable movement toward modern parliamentary government and political democracy. In 1629, Charles dissolved Parliament and ruled without it for eleven years. During those years, the Archbishop of Canterbury was a rigorous high churchman, William Laud. Had it not been for Laud, the Church in Scotland might well have remained episcopal rather than becoming presbyterian.

In 1560, The General Assembly of the Scottish Church broke with Rome and proclaimed a rationally autonomous Scottish Church of which bishops were a part (though their status was somewhat confusing). Charles I had hoped to destroy this Church and establish the Church of England in Scotland, and to this end his Archbishop of Canterbury, William Laud, and John Maxwell, later Bishop of Ross, drew up a prayer book for use in Scotland. This was the book of 1637, and as might be expected, the work was militantly catholic—high church to an extreme. Most Scots rejected both it and the religion it stood for. Religion became an expression of Scottish nationalism and the greater part of Scotland became Presbyterian.

In 1660, Charles II came to the British throne in what history remembers as the Restoration. With the return of the monarchy came the return of the monarch's church, and the Church of England was reestablished. The act by which the church was reestablished also provided a new *Book of Common Prayer*. This was the book of 1662, and it remains the official Prayer Book of the Church of England today. Like earlier editions, it attempted to achieve a balance between extremes. The previous edition of 1559, was distinctly protestant. Moving away from that position, the 1662 book was comparable to the 1552 book in terms of its implicit protestant emphasis. A further attempt at Prayer Book revision in the English Church was made in 1927-1928. The Church's Convocations of York and Canterbury approved the book but Parliament did not, so it occupies a strange, quasi-official status today. It is widely used as a supplement to the official book.

Within the last ten years, revisions have been made. These revisions are in three forms: Series 1-Traditional; Series 2-Contemporary; Series 3-"Experimental." These series are similar to "Holy Eucharist I," "Holy Eucharist II," and "Order for Eucharist," (Rite I, Rite II, and Rite III) as they appear in the *Draft Proposed Book of Common Prayer*.

Anglican Prayer Book worship had a long history by the time it was imported into the American colonies. Its transplanting from England to America was fraught with problems. The Church of England, for example, was highly organized, but in the colonies it was not. Administratively, the colonial Church was under the episcopal supervision of the Bishop of London, who apparently gave little thought to it. No bishops were sent to it. No dioceses were organized, and what organization was discernible was parochial and congregational. This "congregationalism" of *power* has given the Episcopal Church a unique character within the worldwide Anglican Communion and has made it perhaps the most difficult of all Anglican Churches to understand.

Just as Elizabeth I in her day had found public worship to be the only common ground among her subjects, so too worship was the one thing that all Anglicans in colonial America had in common. That a Church whose fiber was knit together with so tenuous a thread as common worship existed at all in amazing. That the Church was able to weather the storm of the American Revolution was an even greater miracle. However hostile was the reception of Anglicanism before the Revolution by colonists whose coming to this continent was inspired by their hatred of it, during the Revolution the situation worsened dramatically. Since the object of the Revolution was to break the hold of the English king, those who esposed the Church of which he was titular head were highly suspect. At what may have been one of the most intensely patriotic and religious periods in American history, the Church of England's feeble strength was sorely tested. When the war ended, most loyalists, the supporters of the British, either went north to Canada or returned to England, and the Church was seriously weakened further.

The Revolution that had made America an independent nation also made the colonial Anglican Church independent. It would have been unthinkable to maintain that the English king was head of it after the Revolution, so it was reorganized in the 1780's. Since it is an Episcopal Church, its first problem was to establish itself within the historic episcopate. With this end in view, a quorum of clergy from Connecticut elected Samuel

82 THE CHURCH IN PERSPECTIVE

Seabury bishop and sent him off to England for consecration by Anglican bishops. The English bishops were unwilling to consecrate Seabury, though, and after he had been put off for some two years, Seabury went to Scotland and there was consecrated at the hands of bishops of the small Scottish Episcopal Church. In gratitude, Bishop Seabury promised to use his influence to bring American Episcopal worship into conformity with that of the Scottish Church. The Prayer Book of the Scottish Church was produced in 1637 under the archepiscopate of the rigid high churchman William Laud.

The first American Prayer Book was the proposed edition of 1785. This was an extremely protestant book, and was never approved for public use. If ever a book was the product of its culture, this one was. The Puritan influence in America was strong. Moreover, the religious climate of the time was deistic and unitarian, and that fact is clearly discernible in the 1785 book. Deism is one of several beliefs which assert fundamentally that God is a creative force who, having brought existence into being, no longer involves himself in it. Unitarianism is the belief that God's being is simple, not complex; that he is not in any sense triune or trinitarian. The Proposed Prayer Book of 1785 conformed to this way of thinking. The Nicene Creed was dropped; the "descensus clause"(that Christ descended in Hell) was deleted from the Apostle's Creed; the Athanasian Creed was dropped, never to be restored. In the services of Morning and Evening Prayer the Gloria Patri after the canticles was dropped. The book was never given official use. The English bishops agreed to consecrate other bishops for America only on the strict assurance of a new edition more appropriate to traditional Anglicanism's middle road position.

In 1789, the First General Convention of the Episcopal Church met in Philadelphia. It approved a new Prayer Book modeled specifically on the 1662 edition of the English Prayer Book, the 1637 Scottish Prayer Book, and the radical 1785 book it was to replace. Since the three books designated as models range from extreme catholic to extreme protestant, a synthesis was effected not unlike that which brought about the English Prayer Book of 1662. Another revision was made in 1892, but this one included few substantive changes. Our present, official, edition of the *Book of Common Prayer* came out in 1928. It was based upon all of the earlier ones and attempted to correct their faults. A notable feature of it is its flexibility and adaptability. It allows much discretion in the lengthening and shortening of services and in their embellishment.

The 1928 edition of the American *Book of Common Prayer* is frequently supplemented by other liturgical books, having various kinds of approval. These include *The Book of Offices*, a collection of extra occasional offices appropriate to such things as Adoption of Children, Setting Apart of Deaconess, Admission of Lay Ministers and Officers, and the like. The supplementary propers, the collects, epistles, and gospels, which are in trial use in the Episcopal Church, are found in a book referred to as *Lesser Feasts and Fasts*. The American Edition of *The People's Anglican Missal* provides the eucharistic rite with special propers, settings, intentions, and instructions pertaining to ceremony. *The Manual for Priests of The American Church* is "complementary to the occasional offices of the Book of Common Prayer"; it is a standard handbook for the forms of auricular confession, benedictions, funeral rites, asperges, consecration of sacred vessels, and so on. In addition, there are countless volumes of prayers. Among the best known are *Prayers New and Old, The Book of English Collects, The Prayer Manual, Pastor's Prayer Book,* and *Prayers for Every Occasion* (Morehouse-Barlow Co.).

A new revision of the American *Book of Common Prayer* is in the making. It has been so for many years, and the preliminary *Prayer Book Studies*, produced by the Standard Liturgical Commission of the General Convention, have culminated in *The Draft Proposed Book of Common Prayer and Other Rites and Ceremonies of the Church*.

What has the Ecumenical Movement meant in terms of Prayer Book revision? Basically, that there are two trends in contemporary liturgical worship: one toward simple relevance and participation, and another toward the broader appreciation of the rich variety inherent in the combined liturgical heritages of Christendom. Dr. Peter Day, the Ecumenical Officer of the Episcopal Church, speaks to this question in the Forward Movement pamphlet entitled, *What About Church Union?* He says, "There is no thought of imposing a new liturgy on any of the congregations of a united Church; accordingly, parishes can go right on using the Prayer Book services to which they are accustomed or to which they will have to become accustomed when the General Convention gets around to taking action on the proposals for revision which are already stirring within the Episcopal Church itself." The Consultation on Church Union, involving several non-Roman communions, including the Episcopal Church, has produced "An Order of Worship" for study.

The Liturgical Movement has already done much to open up the question of corporate worship across denominational lines. Doubtless the ecumenicism with which we are concerned will mean new forms appropriate to a growth in unity and communion. But like all such developments down through history, it will probably be evolutionary and gradual, not revolutionary and precipitous.

IV. THE ECUMENICAL SITUATION

The Disunity of Christians has an ancient history. We have already seen how, in the fourth century, disputes arose with which the General Councils had to deal. From that time on, it has been increasingly difficult for Christians to "agree together in the faith." In the eleventh century, the several separations of the Eastern and Western (i.e., the Orthodox and the Latin) Churches became final and the distinctions formed a line of demarcation. The sixteenth- and seventeenth century Reformation further proliferated and institutionalized different Christian traditions. The Christian church entered the twentieth century with many faces and spoke to the modern world with many voices. The protests of an underlying agreement among the Christian denominations have venerable motives but beg two important questions: their extensive disagreement in matters of faith, and their intensive, often contemptuous rivalry for converts. The differences involve belief, practice, worship, and public and private morality; all denominational differences are held in passionate allegiance to Christ.

Along with this disunion came the ecclesiasticism that expressed it. People began to understand themselves not as followers of Jesus, the Suffering Servant of God, but as Anglicans, or Romans, or Baptists. Membership in the Church meant membership in a competitive denomination with its particular outlook, mentality and individual sense of identity. Institutionalized along the highly competitve and extravagantly expensive lines of prestige and power, the Church became for many an extension of God. To serve God was, for them, to serve the Church.

This kind of thinking easily turned the Church's concerns inward, eroding the true catholicism of *all* Christianity and leaving in place of the inclusiveness of Christian concern an exclusiveness which served the institution but not its Lord. In I Corinthians 12:27, St. Paul describes the Church in a way that implies complete identification with its Lord: "Now you are the Body of Christ and individually members of it." But considering other New Testament metaphors that identify the Church with Christ, and in the light of what St. Paul said it meant for him to belong to Christ, it is plain that he was asserting an identification between individual Christians with their Lord (and thereby with each other). He did not intend the idolatry implied in the twisted notion that, in some mystical sense, the Church is Christ. Subsequent generations have often behaved as though their particular branch of the Church were the whole Church, and the Church itself was, in fact, God. Thus, we came into the twentieth century with Christianity supplanted by a demonic "churchianity" against which Dietrich Bonhoeffer reacted with his predictions of a "religionless Christianity."

Why has the trend now reversed? For one thing, the world in which the denominational situation took shape no longer exists. Indeed, the world in which the theological and liturgical forms with which the Church came to this point in world history no longer exists. The traditional beliefs and practices of Christendom were born in a rural society in which life was short, hard, pervaded with mystery, and relatively dull. Death was an ever-present and grim reality. It was not until the twentieth century that life expectancy in the United States passed the level of forty-five. Now it is about seventy years, and by the year 2000 life expectancy in America may near 135 years. Life is much more comfortable and secure, as well. Most Americans work only seven- or eight-hour days and enjoy frequent holidays. We have been remarkably successful at subduing the earth, as God commanded of our distant ancestors in Old Testament times. In the process of subduing the earth, however, we have replaced many of our prayers with effective, human solutions. Instead of praying that God will spare our children from polio, we vaccinate them. Instead of praying that God will heal our infections, we take antibiotics. Instead of praying that God will send rain, we irrigate and plant hybrid crops tailored to the climate. Instead of praying that God will send us good harvests, we make fertilizers. Instead of praying that God will spare us from the devastation of springtime floods, we build flood basins and dams. Instead of hoping to see relatives in distant countries after we die, we fly to see them in jet planes already operating at such speeds that, at the fortieth parallel of longitude, they can keep pace with the sun! Instead of wondering in childish awe about the moon and the stars, we design space explorations which will extend the world—the place of human dominion, as Genesis uses the word— deep into the universe which we may one day colonize.

Human solutions have replaced many of our parents' prayers, and so God intended it. But in commanding human beings to "subdue the earth," God did not intend to make them the victims of their own success, or to abandon them in their growing maturity and responsibility. God intended people to grow up, to become responsible both for their own history and for the things of nature over which increasingly, they are, stewards. The dignity of humanity consists of responsibility and accountability, and this is what human beings received at God's hands. To possess and exercise responsibility for his personal destiny is to be made in the image of God.

Unfortunately, this is a hard lesson to learn. As we discover ourselves to be the authors of our future history and ever more the controllers of nature's phenomena as well, God's transcendence becomes less and less apparent. God's presence and power and goodness are harder for us to experience within nature and history, and it begins to seem as if God were absent—or even dead. This is important to the Ecumenical Movement because it is the theological statement of a judgment of where humanity is within the comprehensive course of evolution and destiny. If God is increasingly giving into our hands control which was once his alone, then naturally God's transcendence will be increasingly less apparent where once it was so manifest. If, then, God wills to commit to human control nature and history, where shall we look for evidence that God is with us? The answer is the Scriptural one: We shall find God by means of his image, human beings. It is not nature or history that glorify God, for their records are ambiguous. It is people who glorify God in conforming to God's image—which is what it means to be truly human. If we are the Body of Christ, and as such the Church, the Church with which we associate ourselves will understand itself very differently than in the exclusive, narrowly denominational ways of former years. This in fact is just what is happening. This is why humanity's "coming of age" has such enormous and salutary religious significance, and it is one of the reasons why the Ecumenical Movement is important. It is entirely Scriptual that we should "subdue the earth" as we are doing, and that ultimately "there shall be one flock and one Shepherd."

Since no one can write history in advance, predicting the future course of the Ecumenical Movement does not admit the possibility of much detail or precision. It is apparent, though, that if we are clear about where we are in terms of where we started, a *direction* can be identified to indicate where our present ecumenical thinking and involvement is taking us.

The participation of the Episcopal Church in the World Council of Churches and in the National Council of Churches, generally dealt with as ecumenical, are efforts at interdenominational coordination and cooperation and are not ecumenical as such, since they do not have as their ultimate aim the organic unification of participating churches. Because the member Churches of the worldwide Anglican Communion are each nationally independent and autonomous, each pursues its own ecumenical interests. We ought perhaps to have more intra-Anglican ecumenism than we do, for the duplication, competition, and waste of denominationalism invades Anglicanism in the missionary field, where American and English churches fight for survival only blocks apart.

Ecumenical aspirations in the Episcopal Church began over a century ago. In 1853, the Reverend Dr. William A. Muhlenberg and others memorialized General Convention in a document characterizing the Episcopal Church as the instrument for bringing about protestant unity. This move was inspired by two things: the dramatic growth in members of the Roman Catholic Church as a result of the mass immigration of Irish who moved to America after the so-called potato famine of the 1840's, and the increase of unchurched persons among the American citizenry. Although it provoked no direct action, the memorial confronted the Church with its ecumenical ministry. In 1886, the House of Bishops adopted a statement of essentials according to which it felt Episcopalians could discuss church union. The list included the Holy Scriptures as the word of God, the Apostles' and Nicene Creeds, the essentiality of the two sacraments of baptism and communion, and "the doctrine of grace." The great weakness of the memorial was that in calling upon the House of Bishops to extend the ecclesiastical system the bishops then administered to include something "broader and more comprehensive. . . surrounding and including the Protestant Episcopal Church as it now is," they emasculated the essential nature of espiscopacy and assumed an attraction to episcopal obedience by other protestants that simply did not exist. In 1888, the Lambeth Congress, a meeting of bishops representing all the Churches in communion with the Church of England, met and revised the terms of Muhlenberg's memorial in what history recalls as the Chicago-Lambeth Quadrilateral, so that point four concerned not "grace," but the historic episcopate.

The next period of ecumenical encounter came in developments stemming from the pronouncements in the late nineteenth century of the Roman Catholic Church concerning doctrines of the Immaculate Conception of the Blessed Virgin Mary and Papal Infallibility. Not all of the Roman communion found these pronouncements acceptable. The Old Catholic Church in Europe was established at that time by dissenting Roman Catholics and, immediately, various Anglican Churches responded to the Old Catholics with visits and expressions of regard. Gradually, the principle of intercommunion was worked out and, on the basis of it, the American Episcopal Church and the Old Catholic Church entered into full intercommunion in 1940. The relationship is an important one, for though it falls short of organic union, it involves the recognition of each Church's ministry and doctrine. It has formed the basis for similar ecumenical encounters with the Spanish Reformed Church, the Lusitanian Church, and the Philippine Independent Church, all of which entered into full intercommunion with the Episcopal Church in 1961.

Since 1961, our ecumenical endeavors have continued, especially on four fronts: our dialogue with Rome, our dialogue with the Orthodox Churches, our dialogue with the Lutherans, and our participation in the Consultation on Church Union. Perhaps we should consider these in the order in which they are most familiar.

Anglican-Roman relations have warmed considerably since the late Pope John XXIII called the Second Vatican Council to renew and update the Roman communion. The history of Anglican-Roman relations has resembled a sibling rivalry, polarized around two issues but including many others. The two issues are the Anglican denial of papal infallibility and the Roman denial of the validity of Anglican Holy Orders. The doctrine of papal infallibility was declared a matter of essential faith, required to be believed by all Roman Catholics, at the First Vatican Council in 1870. The development of this papal claim has a long and fascinating history. It asserts that when speaking *ex cathedra,* from the chair of Peter, on matters of faith and morals, the pope is under divine inspiration and cannot err. Actually, the doctrine is a little bit of a problem even to Rome, for in the year 634, Pope Honorius I committed heresy while speaking *ex cathedra* on an issue of faith. Roman Catholics have since contended that Honorius was giving a personal opinion, not speaking *ex cathedra* as pope. They may be right, but history records the event as the pope's official ruling. The problem really doesn't involve the papal claim of infallibility, but what that claim means. If the papacy were to understand itself as being no more than the spokesman for the worldwide Roman episcopate—and certainly it is that—and understand its claim of infallibility as the adequate expression of that Church's mind, probably few Christians would take offense. From at least the fifth century, Christians have been disposed to respect a responsible expression of the consensus no matter who speaks it. It is only when viewed as the arbitrary spiritual direction of one man that papal infallibility becomes offensive, and, as such, its days are surely numbered.

As to the denial by Romans of the validity of Anglican Holy Orders, that too has a complex history, and a fascinating one. It wasn't until 1896 that an official papal ruling removed this question from the general area of doctrines in doubt. In that year Pope Leo XIII issued a bull *Apostolicae Curae* pronouncing Anglican Holy Orders "absolutely null and utterly void." Probably, he would never have done so had not English Roman Catholics, whose controversies with the Anglican Church had been especially bitter, insisted on it. Their representative, Cardinal Vaughn, was able to generate enough support for a counter-blow to the then hated Anglicans to accomplish the papal denial of the validity of their ordination. Deferring to the will of those most affected, Leo XIII rendered a judgment enormously expedient, politically astute—and historically absurd. The grounds of denial have shifted over the years since 1896. At present, Rome's denial of the validity of Anglican Holy Orders turns on the question of intention. The intention of Anglican Orders is called defective because no words or actions at ordination seem to confer upon Anglican clergy the power to offer sacrifice. The Archibishops of Canterbury and York replied to this accusation of 1897 by stating precisely how the Anglican Church makes clear its intention to confer upon its ordinands the office instituted by Christ, and how its own doctrine of the eucharistic sacrifice is stated in terms at least as explicitly as those of the Roman mass. Indeed there has been recognition of this by Rome. At the fourth meeting of the Joint Commission on Anglican-Roman Catholic relations in the United States there was thorough consideration of the theology of eucharistic sacrifice. At the end of this meeting, on May 26, 1967, Episcopal Bishop Donald Hallock and Roman Catholic Bishop Charles Hemsing issued a joint statement which said in part, "Since the time of the Reformation, the doctrine of the eucharistic sacrifice has been considered a major obstacle to the reconciliation of the Anglican Communion and the Roman Catholic Church. It is the conviction of our commission that this is no longer true." Like the question of papal infallibility, the question of Rome's conscientious denial of Anglican Holy Orders calls for a clear and acceptable statement of Anglican intention. Hopefully, this generation will see both areas of dissension eliminated.

Another step toward the removal of these impediments to union was taken on March 24, 1966, when the Archbishop of Canterbury and Pope Paul VI made a common declaration of an Anglican-Roman Catholic Joint Preparatory Commission. The Anglican delegation includes theologians from England, Wales, the United States, Canada, Ceylon, and South Africa. The stated purpose of this Commission is the inauguration between the respective communions of a serious dialog which, being based upon gospels and those catholic traditions held in common, may lead to that unity in truth for which Christ prayed. An Anglican Center in Rome has been established and dedicated. Moreover, ecumenical consultations are taking place between the Episcopal Church and the Roman Catholic Church in this country.

These bodies have issued statements including statements on the Eucharist and on the ministry. The statements, along with commentary on them, are published in ARC DOC, I, II, and III.

The Consultation on Church Union grew from four members in 1961 to nine in 1976:

The original four (1961):
 The United Presbyterian Church in the U.S.A
 The Episcopal Church
 The Methodist Church
 The United Church of Christ
Added at the second meeting (1963):
 The International Convention of Christian Churches (Disciples of Christ)
Added at the fifth meeting (1966):
 The Presbyterian Church in the U.S.
 The African Methodist Episcopal Church
Added since the fifth meeting:
 The African Methodist Episcopal Zion Church
 The Christian Methodist Episcopal Church

Our consultations with the Orthodox church have a much longer history and a much less spectacular present. We have long been close to the Orthodox Churches, and with them we are members of the World Council and the National Council of Churches. Long ago, many of the Orthodox Churches went on record as viewing the validity of Anglican Holy Orders in terms entirely equal to Rome's claim of valid Holy Orders. We consult with the Orthodox frequently, cooperate with them in various ways, and enjoy cordial relations, but the main thrust of our own ecumenical endeavors has addressed itself to the reunification of Western Christianity as a prior step to reunification of all Christianity, since Western disunity is 600 years more recent than the East-West schism.

IV. THE ROLE OF THE LAY READER

What It Means to be a Lay Reader

In the Episcopal Church there are approximately 15,000 lay readers. With 6,000 of our approximately 12,000 clergy serving a Church of some 7,000 parishes and missions, two things are apparent: we no longer have a clergy shortage and the need for lay readers has either changed or diminished. Looking at the Church as a whole, it would seem to have changed but not diminished.

When clergy were in short supply, lay readers were frequently needed to substitute for them. With today's abundance of clergy, lay readers are not so much needed to substitute for the clergy as to assist them and to represent the laity's part in the most central functions of the Church's life. There are the exceptional cases in which lay readers still substitute for the clergy, such as in small, rural missions too poor to support their own clergy and too remote to be incorporated into a neighboring mission, and, again, in the absence or illness of the clergy in a typical small parish. Usually, though, the need is for the assistance of lay readers.

According to the national Canon Law of the Episcopal Church (Title III-Canon 25, Sec.1), a lay reader is "a competent person" licensed by a bishop to conduct public worship by reading only the following offices and observing the limitations indicated.:

(1) Morning and Evening Prayer, omitting the Absolution, unless using Proposed Prayer Book (see *Guide for Lay Readers*);
(2) The Litany;
(3) The Penitential Office;
(4) The Offices of Instruction;
(5) In the Order for Holy Communion, The Epistle only unless using Proposed Prayer Book, then entire pro-anaphora is read (see *Guide for Lay Readers*);
(6) The Burial Offices; substituting for the priestly blessing the concluding prayer at the end of the Shorter Form for Family Prayer at Evening; substituting for the priestly blessing at the grave the final prayer at the end of the Shorter Form for Family Prayer at Morning; and substituting for the priestly blessing at the Burial of a Child the concluding prayer at the end of the Shorter Form for Family Prayer at Evening.

Also, "He shall not deliver Sermons or addresses of his own composition, unless, after instruction and examination, he be specially licensed thereto by the Bishop" (Sec. 4). The most recent provision says, further, "A Lay Reader may deliver the Cup at the Holy Communion; *Provided*, that he has been specially licensed thereto by the Bishop" (Sec. 5).

These limitations sound stringent, but two examples of abused lay reader status will show why they exist. There are some states in which one may set up as a marriage counselor with neither training nor experience in that field. Such people can do enormous harm. One such person carried on marriage counseling practice for several years. Finally his "depth conference" got one of his clients into such distress that the marriage counselor was asked by a relative for his credentials. At this point, the marriage counselor blandly explained that he was licensed by his church. The incredulous questioner (not an Episcopalian) asked to see the counselor's license. Finally, it came out that an Episcopal lay reader's license was all the marriage counselor had. This is an extreme case and the fraudulence implied hardly calls for comment. Needless to say, the bishop did not allow the reader to retain his license.

The second example involves a lay reader's well-meant incompetence. He was preaching at a small mission when my wife and I, traveling, dropped in for Sunday morning worship. The sermon was a scandal, no less for its syntax than its theology. The lay reader was preaching about the "homobusion" (sic), a word he had almost learned somewhere and decided he must share with fellow worshipers. His point was that Christ actually was God and man—"half divine and half human." My wife dissuaded me from rising to my feet and restating his proposition. After the service, I asked the lay reader if he had written his own sermon, and he told me he wouldn't be so presumptuous; what he had done was to rewrite one of the Church's *Lay Reader Sermons* to make it clearer for the congregation!

Obviously, the two lay readers in these examples were woefully ignorant of what it means to be a lay reader. Traditionally, lay readers have had a very important ministry in this country. In colonial times, when clergy were scarce, the lay reader was held in deference equal to that usually reserved for the clergy. Many founded congregations, some of which are flourishing parishes to this day. In colonial times, during special emergencies, lay readers baptized, heard confessions, even pronounced absolutions and benedictions. They mediated grace and comfort to the dying, the bereaved, the sick, the penitent, the lonely, and the insecure. In the early days of colonial America, they were among the few religious leaders the Church had, for as the Church of America remained officially a part of the Church of England, it was under the jurisdiction of the Bishop of London, and he did little for it. As we have already observed, no bishops were sent to reside in America to guide the growth and work of the young church, and it was forced to organize itself along somewhat congregational lines. Because its work did not appeal to the capable among English clergy, a "clergy shortage" of serious proportions came into being and lay readers became crucially important to the Anglican population.

Today, the lay reader's role is less clear. What is clear is that, whereas he once literally had to *substitute* for a priest, he generally serves now as an *assistant* to the priest. To be sure, he frequently functions where the priest is not present—in nursing homes, jails, small missions, and the like—but he is nearly always working in a situation in which ordained clergy are ultimately responsible for what he does. The confusion focused on the role of lay readers is manifest in the diverse standards of training and licensing that apply to them.

The Episcopal Church is that branch of the worldwide Anglican Communion under the leadership of the Presiding Bishop and in communion with the Triennial General Convention. It is a confederation of over a hundred autonomous dioceses, each of which has canonical responsibility for the training, licensing, and supervision of its lay readers. Although Canon 49 of the Church Canons sets forth the general and national standards for lay reader training, each diocese has such latitude in the interpretation and application of this particular canon that, operationally, no two dioceses have been alike. This means two things: there are as many standards for lay reader training as there are dioceses and what it means to be a lay reader in one of our dioceses in likely to be very different from what it means to be a lay reader in another. Lay reading tends to differ as much from one place to another as life does. Thus the lay reader in Honolulu may be in a different situation entirely from the lay reader in Massachusetts. As the trend of frequent moves by Americans has increased in recent years, so too has the problem of diverse lay reader training standards.

At the General Convention of 1964, the canon regulating the training and licensing of readers was revised. Implied in the rewriting of Canon 49 was recognition of the need for further reform along the lines of training and function. By defining the standards for a diocesan lay reader, the canon attempted to set standards for all lay readers qualified to take charge of a mission which would be both uniform and minimal among all the dioceses. It is these uniform, minimum standards which this *Standard Lay Reader's Training Course* attempts to meet. It is hoped that this uniform minimum training will recover, where it has been lost for lay readers, their traditional work of Christian education and missionary outreach.

An unfortunate, complicating factor in the reform of lay reader training and service is a controversy having to do with the relative appropriateness of lay readers on the one hand and the diaconate on the other. This is a highly refined form of clergy-laity conflict. Lay readers are, of course, laymen, and deacons are clergy, yet, except that deacons can read the Gospel at Holy Communion, their functions are identical.

The probability for the future is that the lay reader's role will develop as new ways are found for effective participation in the Church's ministry. Probably the industrial mission will make use of lay readers as the best connective between the Church, which is residential and oriented toward people's leisure time activity, and the business world, in which people spend some of their most important hours, make decisions with far-reaching significance, and find their religious self-expression most difficult.

Practical Tips for the Lay Reader*

I. *The Conduct of Public Worship*

The lay reader, particularly a new one, should review the services (with appropriate adaptations) he is licensed to conduct. These are set forth in this manual on page 96 and in Canon 49 of the national Canons. He should also study carefully the rubrics (the regulations printed in small type) in the *Book of Common Prayer* or *The Draft Proposed Book of Common Prayer* pertaining to the service or the portion of service the lay reader intends to conduct. These rubrics should be reviewed every time a lay reader is going to lead or assist in the conduct of public worship.

If the lay reader is assisting a clergyman, he is required to conform to the instructions of the clergy even if those instructions do not conform to the rubrics. Clergy have a certain latitude of discretion in these matters, which is generally regulated by the bishop, and the lay reader can, therefore, defer to the instructions of the priest or bishop without anxiety of conscience.

Whether conducting an entire service or only a portion thereof, the lay reader should *practice his entire part aloud*, preferably in the place where the service will be held. Most lay readers are unaccustomed to projecting their voices and are therefore not heard. This matter of voice projection is especially important if the congregation includes older people whose hearing may not be good. It is also important to read slowly. "Stage fright" is normal even for the most experienced clergy, and the anxiety that one normally feels tends to make

---

*For more information, see also the *Guide for Lay Readers* (Morehouse-Barlow Co., New York), available at church bookstores, or directly from the publisher (78 Danbury Rd., (Rte 8), Wilton, Conn. 06897).

him race through the service, which makes it difficult to to undertand and follow. Deliberately, make yourself read slowly enough so that it feels too slow. Then your reading rate will be about right. Anything over 120 words a minute is too fast.

II. Planning a Service

Some rules apply whether the service is to be held in the church or in some other facility:

a) Determine on which day of the Church year the service is to be held. This can be done by checking a liturgical calendar (like *The Christian Planning Calendar* or *The Episcopal Church Calendar*) or telephoning a neighboring clergyman of the diocesan office and explaining that you don't have a church calendar and need to know in order to prepare a service. Next, if the service is Morning or Evening Prayer, select the psalm or psalms and the lessons. This is done by looking them up in the front of the *Book of Common Prayer* (pages x-xlv), in the *Draft Proposed Prayer Book* (pages 888-1001), or in one of the calendars. Sometimes, particularly on Sundays, you will have a choice. If you have a short sermon, one of the longer psalms or even two, as well as the longer lessons, may be appropriate. Read the psalms and lessons over quickly and see what they are about. Once you know this you can select hymns (if you don't leave that task to the organist) that have the same subject or emphasis. (The Episcopal Church Calendar mentioned above has complete suggestions for hymns.)

You will select your hymns from the hymnal. Notice that it is arranged in several seasons. Select simple hymns that are familiar to the people and give a list of them to the organist well in advance. Some organists may be prepared to play anything on a moment's notice, but most will appreciate having a week in which to prepare the music. You will need three hymns: a processional, a sermon hymn, and a recessional.

Now write your order of service, based on the rubrics and general custom. Although the **Prayer Book** allows several variants in conducting each service, it is best to use one simple form of service with which you are familiar, until you have become accustomed to it. Your order for Morning Prayer will look something like this if you use the 1928 *Book of Common Prayer*

Organ Prelude (organist makes selection)	
Processional Hymn	
Opening Sentences	pp.3-5
Exhortation (Short Form, p.6, or Long Form, p.5)	
General Confession (but omit The Declaration of Absoltion, p.7)	p.6
The Lord's Prayer	p.7
The Versicles ("O Lord, open thou our lips...")	p.7
The Gloria Patri ("Glory be to the Father....")	p.8
The Invitation (as appropriate)	p.8
The Venite	p.9
The Gloria Patri	p.9
Psalm(s), each followed by the Gloria Patri (p.9)	
The First Lesson (see Prayer Book, pp x-xlv, or calendar for selections)	
A Canticle (*Te Deum laudamus*, or *Benedictus es, Domine*, or *Benedicite, omnia opera Domini*)	pp.10-13
The Gloria Patri	p.9
The Second Lesson	p.15
A Canticle (*Benedictus* or *Jubilate Deo*)	pp.14-15
The Gloria Patri	p.9
The Apostles Creed (or The Nicene Creed)	p.15
Salutation and Versicles ("The Lord be with you....")[1]	p.16
Collect for the Day (On a saint's day or other special day, the special collect for the occasion is read first, followed by the proper collect for that day)	pp.90-265

---

1. In a shortened service the Lord's Prayer, p.7, will come at this point; see second rubric, p.16.

Collects for Peace and Grace[2]   p.17
Other prayers (optional)   pp.17-18
A General Thanksgiving   p.19
A Prayer of St. Chrysostom   p.20
The Grace   p.20
Announcements
Sermon Hymn
The Sermon
Offertory Sentences (selected)
The Offering (appropriate anthem such as "Praise God, from whom all blessings flow..." or "All things come of thee, O Lord..." sung by minister or choir)
Recessional Hymn
Closing Prayer (optional, As candles are being extinguished the lay reader may read the third collect, p. 49, beginning "Grant, we beseech thee, Almighty God...")

In addition to the forms of service in the Standard (1928) Prayer Book, you will need to become familiar with the revised forms in the *Draft Proposed Book of Common Prayer*. It allows you considerable choice which the present Prayer Book does not permit of contain[3]

The order for any service may be worked out from rubrics in whichever Prayer Book you use, as the above order was prepared, and with help, if necessary, from a neighboring

---

2. The rubrics permit the service to be concluded after this point with other "general intercessions" from the Prayer Book, or directly with the Grace, though usually the prayers on pages 17-20 are used, at least in part.

3. A complete manual for determining the order of service for Morning and Evening Prayer, as well as other services a lay reader may perform, is in the *Guide for Lay Readers* (rev. ed.) prepared by The General Division of Laymen's Work (Morehouse-Barlow Co., New York), Chapter 5, "Order and Conduct of the Services," and Appendix III.

clergyman. If the service is held outside the church, the service should be adapted as necessary. In a nursing home, for example, one will omit processions and simply announce the nymns. There would probably be no offertory. If you are asked to take a service in an interdenominational setting, remember that you have been asked as an Episcopalian and do as you normally do. No one will be offended. Don't try to compose a pan-Protestant or a Protestant-Catholic service. You will only wish you hadn't—and so will everybody else.

III. *Service Arrangements:*

Plan to arrive at the place of worship at least forty minutes before the service. This will allow you to vest at a relaxed pace, to review in your mind what you will do (and when), and generally to compose yourself. Morevouer, it will give you time to deal with last-minute emergencies.

Give a list of hymns to the organist at least a day early if you can, or let the organist select them with you so that they are in keeping with the season and the theme of the lessons and sermon. If you are conducting a service in a church building, see that it is unlocked. Candles must be lit. Do it early or have an acolyte do it ten minutes before the service begins. Are the flowers on the altar? Have you looked up and marked the lessons in the lectern Bible? Are the lights on? The heat? If the weather is warm, are windows open?

In general, the same rules apply even if the service is held in a prison, a hospital, a nursing home, or somewhere else. Organize the service well ahead of time and coordinate what you are going to do with everyone else having a special part. Surprises during a service of worship are enormously distracting. If something does go wrong, don't lose your poise. Calm dignity can cover the largest of errors and make them unnoticeable to any but the most astute.

IV. Preparing Candidates for Confirmation

The first question one faces in respect to confirmation is, who is eligible? There are two criteria according to which this is determined: age and whether or not the candidate has been already confirmed by a bishop in the line of Apostolic Succession. Your bishop will establish the confirmation age in your diocese (he has considerable discretionary power in this), and he will inform you about any doubtful cases of prior confirmation. Persons once confirmed by a bishop in the line of historic Apostolic Succession (e.g., Roman Catholics, some Lutherans, etc.) are not reconfirmed when they join the Episcopal Church; they are received. So if there is any question as to whether a person desiring to join the Episcopal Church should be confirmed or received, refer the matter to your bishop for a judgement. In any case, all candidates for membership in the Episcopal Church, whether by confirmation or reception, receive the same confirmation instruction contained in the Offices of Instruction in the Prayer Book (p.283) or the Catechism (pp. 844-862) in the *Draft Proposed Prayer Book*.

What should confirmation instruction be in terms of content and method? What preparation is required? Again to refer to page 283 of the Prayer Book, the Offices of Instruction contain the *minimum* required for confirmation. The lay reader looking ahead to preparing confirmands should study this section of the Prayer Book thoroughly, and he ought not to lose sight of the fact that the Offices of Instruction are *minimum statements* of what an adult Christian ought to know. In terms of what it is desirable to confirmands to know, the catechist (or teacher of catechumens, which is the proper word for a candidate for confirmation) might well make use of material from sections I-IV of this book. The material would need some adaptation, of course, but the teachers of confirmation class may use it freely. For permission to reproduce any of it, however, the publisher must be consulted. Other resources for the preparation of confirmands are available through church channels. There are parish, diocesan, or national church sources and publishing houses such as Morehouse-Barlow Co. and Seabury Press.

Confirmation instruction should, under normal circumstances, be at least one hour per week for 12 weeks. Classes of over and hour are too long for 12-14 year old children. Although more than one session a week is sometimes a possibility, generally speaking, the hour a week schedule has been found to be best. The question of whether or not to have separate sessions for adults and children always comes up. My own feeling is that it is better to have adults and children in class together. The Church has been guilty at times of allowing its people to think of Christian education as some kind of youth activity. To dispel this notion, young people must be made to feel their oneness with the adults, so putting them in class together has more to commend it than separation—even if there is only one adult involved! Incidentally, the presence of adult students envokes interest and tends to insure order in the class.

Before scheduling confirmation instruction, arrange a confirmation date with your bishop. This is important for assuring the class that they have a goal twelve weeks off. Goals are important and getting to them is half the fun. In setting the date, be sure to set the *place*. If it is not at your own church, it may be at a neighboring parish. In any event, don't take for granted that you know where the bishop is planning to confirm your class. When the day approaches, see that your vestments are in order, and rehearse the presentation of confirmands to the bishop (*Book of Common Prayer*, p. 296) with your class.

V. *The Lay Pastorate*

For lay readers today, the pastoral side of their work will generally involve them in two kinds of work. Many lay readers choose not to develop strictly pastoral contacts, and in certain dioceses bishops or supervising clergy strictly forbid them to do so. Wherever you serve, therefore, you must be sure that lay readers in your locale are or can be authorized to pursue a pastoral ministry before you attempt to develop one. Most bishops and clergy will greet inquirers of this sort with sympathy and even gratitude, so don't hesitate to make your wishes known. After all, the entire body of Episcopal clergy equals less than one-quarter of one percent of the Church's membership, and most clergy can use all the help they can get.

The lay pastorate generally involves *calling*. There are two kinds—parish calling and sick calling. The purpose of parish calling is to develop a climate of confidence, fellowship, and support within which the Church's ministry can flourish. It is public relations in the best sense—public relations for Christ. In making a parish call, you assure people of the Church's and its Lord's concern for them and for their well-being. Your message is basically that the parish family isn't complete without the person you are calling on. The Church takes the position (and has done ever since our Lord's Parable of the Lost Sheep, Matthew 18:12; Luke 15:3) that the Church has a stake in each of its members, and has none to spare. People are individually priceless in God's eyes. So true is this that when, for humanity's sake, Christ was of more use to God in dying than in living, Christ accepted his Father's will and embraced a shameful death so that others would be saved. That was his ministry, and our ministry is his ministry also. The Christian family is not complete so long as one of God's precious ones is lost.

Another aspect of parish calling is to consult people. It is to inform them of what the Church sees its mission to be and how important their support of that mission is. The Church is a fellowship whose concerns are redemption and reconciliation. It can only do what its members will support it in doing, however, and it has no supporters to spare. Even if we feel we must at some point oppose its program, our opposition ought, for Christ's sake, to be at least *loyal opposition.*

There are some tips that may be helpful: (1) Err in the direction of courtesy—don't take offense if you run into opposition; you don't have to make the world safe for God. (2) If you live in an urban area, don't drop in on people without telling then ahead of time that you are going to do so. (3) Decide ahead of time on one topic you want to emphasize. (4) Get their opinions about it. (5) A few weeks later, tell them how their views have been important in terms of parish planning.

Sick calling is completely different from parish calling. The purpose is centered entirely upon the patient's need. You are there as an audiovisual aid for God. Your presence symbolizes his presence and care and love. Just as in parish calling, there are some principles worth remembering:

(1) If the patient is in a hospital or nursing home, telephone the institution and ask when you can best make a *pastoral call* outside of regular visiting hours. Probably, they will ask you to come at the end of a regular visiting hour. Don't insist on privacy, but avoid busy visiting hours.

(2) Don't stay too long; fifteen minutes is plenty and twenty minutes may be too long. After all, sick people are emotionally, as well as physically, weak.

(3) Tell the patient who you are. For example: "I'm John Doe; I'm a lay reader at St. Peter's Church. We're sorry to hear that you've been sick, and we hope at least you're recovering comfortably."

(4) Be cheerful (or stay away). Even if the patient is dying, you can reassure him or her that some of the best medical care is available.

(5) Ask if there is anything you can do to make the person more comfortable. Can you arrange for a priest to bring Communion?

(6) By this time the patient may be moved to talk a bit. If so, *listen quietly.* If you can't answer a question, say so. For example: "I don't know a great deal of theology, but I know that God has contributed a lot to my happiness and stability, and I believe he provides for other people's needs in the same way." Don't get in over your depth. If someone wants a priest get one. Call the diocesan office for advice if necessary. And if it's the best you can do, call an ordained clergyman of another

faith.

(7) When you are ready to leave ask "What's your first name?" Then say, "John, I'm going to keep you in my prayers, and if you will just lie back and close your eyes, I'll begin here with you." Then stand by his bed and either take one of his hands in yours or lay a hand on his forehead and recite the prayer "For the Recovery of A Sick Person" on page 597 of the Prayer Book. Then leave. Try to say the prayer from memory—it means more than if it's read.

VI. *The Lay Reader in Charge of a Mission*

The lay reader in charge of a mission will need to obtain discreet instruction from the bishop appointing him as to whether he or the warden will preside at meeting of the Board of Advice. It is possible that he won't even be a member of the board, and since he is the bishop's appointee, as St. Ignatius advised eighteen centuries ago, he should do nothing without the bishop's instructions in the matter. Equally important, he should respect the authority of the mission's warden.

The thing every lay reader certainly needs to know is how to plan a funeral. The rules are as follows (make a note of them in the back of your Prayer Book for ready reference):

(1) When you take charge of your mission, instruct the people that, in the event of a death, they should call you at once. Funerals should conform to the tradition and practice of the church. If you are faced with this situation, call the bishop or your supervising priest.

(2) When a death occurs and you are summoned, go immediately to the bereaved and offer your sympathy. Assure them that you will keep them and their departed loved one in your prayers, and say that you would like to begin now. Tell them to relax and close their eyes and pray with you. The say the prayer "For an Anniversary of One Departed" on page 598 of the Prayer Book. Then read the prayer on page 336 beginning "Most merciful Father..." and close with "The Grace of our Lord Jesus Christ, etc."

110 THE CHURCH IN PERSPECTIVE

(3) Now the legal and funeral details have to be worked out. Has a doctor signed a death certificate? If not, call their family doctor (don't call yours, call theirs). If the death appears to be suicidal or otherwise violent, the pronouncing doctor will have to call the police, who send the coroner and conduct and investigation. Cooperate fully and willingly with the medical and legal authorities. They have serious responsibilities which deserve your full respect and cooperation; not to cooperate may be a criminal offense.

(4) When you have medical clearance (and legal, if death is suspicious or violent), the body may be removed. Pending clearance, an undertaker should be selected and alerted. When clearance for removal is obtained from the doctor (and, if necessary, the police), tell the undertaker to remove the body. Stay with the bereaved to support them.

(5) After you have done all you can for the bereaved, suggest a rest and leave. Promise to return in a few hours or the next day to plan the funeral.

(6) Funeral arrangements are always complicated. Many people are involved beside the undertaker, but none should be more actively involved than you. Here's what to do:

(a) Call the undertaker and schedule a meeting with yourself and the next of kin who will actually pay for the funeral.
(b) Go to the family of the deceased and inquire if members are able to proceed with the arrangements. Most people are anxious to settle them. Help to obtain any information they need.
(c) See if the deceased owns a grave plot or has access to one, and if a will or letter has been left by the deceased stating his or her own wishes in the matter. If so, try to follow them; if not,
(d) State the Church's position on funerals. The Church encourages its people to hold funerals in the church. This is a question of what is appropriate, but if the deceased is an atheist, or there are other considera-

The Role of the Lay Reader   111

tions, the funeral home will do. Don't make an issue; simply suggest it. The Church also discourages viewing. Respect the feelings of the bereaved, however. *Don't allow the casket to be open during the funeral service itself.* The Church encourages economy in funerals. Ask what the bereaved can afford (there is a $400 burial allowance for people on social security, and members of fraternal orders are sometimes eligible for assistance). Check out these possible sources of assistance. *Set a total figure for all terminal expenses,* including removal, embalming, casket, grave plot, grave opening or cremation, hearse rental, flowers, organist and sexton, newspaper obituaries, etc. To be realistic, it will probably be at least $700 for a burial, $400-500 for a cremation as a decent option to burial. In establishing a total figure for all terminal expenses, you will be assisting the funeral director, for no ethical undertaker wishes to bankrupt his clients.

(e) Now, accompany the next of kin to the funeral director's office and make the arrangements. They will have decided on cremation or burial. Tell the funeral director what is desired and the total amount of money available for terminal expenses. The ask for an itemized statement. This is important. Don't sign anything for the next of kin. Legally, they must sign in order to be responsible for the expense.

(7) Possible economies are many:

(a) You don't need to use a hearse. A funeral station wagon can be used discreetly. If so, have the body brought to the Church an hour and a half before the service (if the service is not a memorial service), and in the funeral ask the congregation to remain seated until the candles are extinguished, then don't extinguish the candles until the funeral vehicle has left for the

112 THE CHURCH IN PERSPECTIVE

       cemetery or crematorium. Make sure the funeral director understands these arrangements and that he is to take the body to the cemetary or crematory before the people leave the church, not in a motor procession.
- (b) You need not invest in an expensive casket, and the Church discourages extravagant caskets. When the casket is in the Church, have it covered with a pall (even if you have to borrow one) or a bed sheet dyed black or purple (you can get this done quite easily). Under a pall, all caskets look alike.
- (c) You should know that burial vaults may not be required by law.
- (d) If cremation precedes a memorial service, a pine box will do for a casket, and it is probably more appropriate to the purpose.

(8) Plan the service carefully, following the rubrics. Read it slowly. Have hymns if the bereaved wish them. If the deceased was an atheist or non-Christian, do not use the Burial Office from the Prayer Book, use the service from *The Manual for Priests*, omitting absolutions and benedictions. At any burial, when you reach the cemetery you may ask God's blessing on the grave, using the appropriate form from *The Book of Offices*.

(9) Frequently, when cremation is used, a memorial service is held in place of a funeral. The memorial service uses the same burial office and the ashes may or may not be present. Ashes do not have to be buried. They may be kept by the next of kin or the undertaker or (where law permits) scattered in a garden of remembrance (which is probably best).

(10) After the service, record it as you would any other service in the mission's Service Register.

Another thing every lay reader need to know is how to administer emergency baptism. This is explained in the *Book of Common Prayer* on page 281 under the heading "Private Baptism." Instructions for administering emergency baptism are to be found on pages 315-316 of the *Draft Proposed Prayer Book*. Be familiar with the one you will be most likely to be using. When you are called on, it may be too late for you to do your homework. Record it in the parish registry and inform the bishop of the circumstances, person, sponsor(s), etc. *In extreme situations* you may be the sponsor and your saliva the water. Lick your thumb discreetly and make the sign of the cross three times as indicated.

Finally, there is the matter of how to establish a new mission. All you need to know is what your bishop's wishes and instructions are. Refer the matter to him and defer to his judgement.